Silence
Everyday Living and Praying

Silence
Everyday Living and Praying

Joyce Ann Zimmerman, CPPS

LITURGY
TRAINING
PUBLICATIONS

In accordance with c. 827, permission to publish is granted on March 9, 2010, by Very Reverend John F. Canary, Vicar General of the Archdiocese of Chicago. Permission to publish is an official declaration of ecclesiastical authority that the material is free from doctrinal and moral error. No legal responsibility is assumed by the grant of this permission.

Printed in the United States of America.

Library of Congress Control Number: 2009943111

ISBN 978-1-56854-902-6

ESELP

Contents

Introduction

Why in this world would I write a book on silence? How counter-cultural! How daunting! How needful! Yes, needful. For many of us silence is a luxury—perhaps we might grab a bit of it before we head out the door for work in the morning, or we might enjoy a little silence in those never-never-land moments before we fall exhausted into sleep at night. If the baby is colicky, we might sigh in relief at the few seconds of silence between outbursts, or if our heads are spinning from trying to sort out three people talking to us at once, we might welcome being paged with its polite opportunity to excuse ourselves.

Few of us think very much about silence or that we might actually *need* it in order to live more healthy, balanced, productive lives. But to deepen our spiritual lives, especially do we need silence. In fact, without silence our spiritual lives become as noisy and bothersome as so much of our everyday lives. Silence is about living and praying what is truly a *sacred art*. Silence is *sacred* because it lifts us up out of the ordinary; takes us out of ourselves; enables us to focus on our deepest values, desires, and aspirations. Silence is *art* because it frees us for new possibilities and insights; prepares us for the unexpected and extraordinary; draws forth from us that which is wholly new, unintended, and liberating.

It is too easy a way out to blame our world—society and culture and lifestyle—for the lack of silence in our everyday living. True, it is difficult to be in our countries, cities, workplaces, play places, and homes today and find any kind of real silence. The sounds (mostly just noise) of vehicles, machinery, entertainment, communication, and myriads of other things all carelessly flood upon us night and day. That is society's contribution to the sound-noise around us. But this really is not where my interest in silence lies, nor is it the source of my desire to write this book.

The lack of silence in our lives most often lies within ourselves and we ourselves are the real culprits. Many times we might actually seek the sound-noises all around us, making sure every moment is filled with them. We tend to run from silence because, innately, we know that silence wakes us to newer dimensions of ourselves and dares us to delve deeper into the recesses of mystery. Silence never leaves us satisfied with ourselves or with our relationships with others. Silence has the uncanny knack for alerting us to things about ourselves and others we might wish to avoid admitting or confronting. Silence always challenges us to change. Silence can be daunting enough when we are alone, and almost unbearable when we are with others.

At the same time, when a deep silence is an abiding part of self and everyday living and praying, peace and tranquility mark us. Insight and encounter are frequently its fruits. When a deep silence is experienced with others, its fruit is interpersonal communion. There is a satisfaction with the other which rests in sheer delight with the goodness and dignity of the other. This kind of silence is explosive and rewarding. So, here we have it: silence both scares us and attracts us.

This book is about silence—living and praying it as a truly sacred art. My own life experience has convinced me that we must have regular periods of silence in our everyday lives if we are to grow as fulfilled human beings and if we are to grow deeper in our spiritual communion with each other and God. Doctors and other experts might show that silence is helpful for psychological and emotional health, and even for physical health since silence can relax and heal the body. All this is well and good, and in the chapters that follow we obliquely refer to these areas. The goal of this book, however, is ultimately directed to spiritual insight and growth. This is not merely a self-help book. It is primarily intended to be a book about prayer and a prayer book.

I've never sat down to write a book before, knowing both so much and so little about its subject. Some of my friends asked me how in the world I could write book-length words about silence. As I began writing, I didn't have a whole lot of words at hand, but I did have a good long life of experiences to feed me. So, I sat and reflected on my experiences, and found myself praying. The words, then, have come out of my praying—my encounters and conversations with the Divine One who always speaks so eloquently with us when we take the time to quiet ourselves and be attentive. I prayed this book into existence. I can only pray that those who read it pray themselves more deeply into existence, learning to appreciate ever more greatly the great gift silence is, for both our everyday living and praying.

How This Book Works

The structure of the book unfolds in two parts, with two chapters as bookends. An initial bookend (chapter 1) situates us in the mystery and awe of silence and explores why I wish to speak of silence as a sacred art. A feature begun in this first chapter and continued throughout the book is one I have termed "Reader

Response Interlude." These are recurring opportunities for the reader to make personal the text and take time to savor the text in terms of everyday living and prayer. This feature tags regular places in the text where the reader is invited to stop, ponder, and be silent. From the very beginning, therefore, this book is as much a text leading to contemplation and prayer as it is a manual for everyday living of silence.

Part 1 consists of two more generalized chapters treating silence and everyday living. After spending some time thinking about how frenetic our lives are and how silence can lead us to make other choices that bring us to greater calm (chapter 2), chapter 3 takes us through some specific exercises to help us understand the value of and human need for silence. In this chapter silence is explored as a way of life and as an ascetical practice. Part 2 shifts specifically to exploring silence as an aid for prayer or, indeed, as a kind of prayer in itself. Here the real value of silence comes to the fore as an essential component of prayer and worship (chapters 4, 5, and 6).[1]

Finally, we conclude with the other bookend: chapter 7 is a brief reflection on silence as essential for a faith-filled believer living in peace and justice. In this way we are poignantly reminded that while silence has enormous benefits for us personally, in order to be fully fruitful, the art of silence must always lead outside of ourselves toward the good and well-being of others.

This book includes both reflection content and practice exercises for exploring how silence might become an everyday habit—a habit undertaken out of a sense of commitment and need. The reflections are intended to win over the reader to the need for silence in everyday living or strengthen the reader's conviction about the benefits of the habit of silence if the habit is already a part of his or her daily living. The many exercises are intended to help one form the habit (or deepen the habit) of silence which fosters a healthy lifestyle and fruitful prayer. Points of reflection (Reader Response Interlude) spur readers to think beyond the page to their own lives and encounter others and God in a most likely place—in the singular solitude of silence.

With Thanks . . .

I never dreamed of writing a book on silence. Only with the enthusiasm and encouragement of others has this book come to fruition. First, I owe a debt of gratitude to my late mother who taught me so well to seek silence at even a tender young age. She herself was a woman of both deep silences and eloquent words. When I answered God's call to religious life and entered the Sisters of the Precious Blood at Dayton, Ohio, little did I know that learning their spirituality and discipline in silence would carry me so well through whatever life offered me. I would like to thank Nathan Bierma, the communications and research coordinator for the Calvin Institute of Christian Worship in Grand Rapids, Michigan, who invited me to write up some brief comments I made about silence at Calvin College for the CICW Web site. That invitation afforded me my first attempt to put into words what had been lurking so many years in my heart. For that, I will be ever grateful beyond words. Finally, I owe a debt of gratitude to editor Danielle Knott of Liturgy Training Publications; her enthusiasm about the manuscript was encouraging, and her patience with all my questions and concerns was sensitive, and her care through the editing process was heart-warming. Thank you, one and all.

NOTE

1. The reflections and prayer invitations comprising chapter 6 draw specifically from the scriptures. This doesn't mean, however, that others of completely different faith persuasions would not necessarily benefit from them. Readers might wish to substitute sacred writings of their own traditions when different from these given, or use favorite passages, drawing on the method used in the 15 reflections and prayers given in this chapter.

CHAPTER I

Silence—a Sacred Art

I gained an equally healthy respect for the notion that the real story is often found not in the noise but in the silence—and that is why it is so often missed.[1]

As I begin this first chapter of our journey together into the silence as living and praying a sacred art, I am distracted by a late summer thunderstorm raging outside my window. What I discover myself feeling and experiencing in those seconds between the flaming flash of lightning bolt and the growling clap of thunder is what this book tries to describe. As the storm bears down ever closer and closer, the seconds between lightning and thunder decrease. Now, with the full fury of the storm upon me, I find myself holding my breath in between the sight and sound in dreaded anticipation. My head tells me it is the lightning that can hurt me (a few years ago a bolt struck a tree twenty feet from my apartment, and I lost all my electronics in one fell swoop!), but I still wait during that tiny instant with bated breath for the thunder. Then I *feel* in my bones the deep rumble which resonates in my head. The lightning causes me to blink; the thunder, to shudder. As I reflect on those in-between seconds betwixt blink and shudder, I am aware of experiencing a profound kind of silence filled with awe, fascination, anticipation.

It is not in the noise of the storm that I find the real story of who I am in terms of my relation to the larger canvas of cosmos and ultimate life meaning, but in that brief, insightful instant of silence when I am so aware of myself and what I am feeling. And isn't this what we all seek—to know who we are? Lest we forget who we are, we are given these precious moments throughout life when we are brought up short by the breathless instants of absolute silence, when we are stripped of all pretensions and distractions and simply encounter ourselves in the vastness of nothingness and possibilities. It is here, in these times of silence, that we might also be brought to the sacred, and this is the real story we seek: to meet our Creator.

No, it is not in sound-noise that we encounter the sacred, but in silence—that in-between time when we hold our breath because something powerful and ever wonderful is anticipated. Perhaps this is why I have chosen to write this book:

I always experience profound, sacred silence as a moment[2] filled with awe, fascination, anticipation. No matter how we name our God, in silence we strip away all pretensions which keep us from encountering God in power and glory, and also in gentleness and compassion.

Nevertheless, encountering God is not the only *sacred* moment—any kind of experience of someone or something beyond ourselves can be sacred. That precious moment when a young couple looks into each other's eyes and love stirs strongly can be a sacred moment. So can the reverence new parents feel when they hear the first cry of their newborn. So can the glory of a magnificent sunrise, when the whole world seems to be washed afresh with life. Our life is scattered with sacred moments—those hallowed times which bring us up short, cause us to face ourselves and others in honesty and boldness and wonder, and bring to the fore our deepest meaning and values. The challenge is to recognize sacred moments for what they are and allow these moments to bring us consciously to the brink of mystery and wonder.

When we become conscious of sacred moments and the attendant process of encountering the sacred through silence, this process is truly an *art*—the deliberate human production of something beautiful. Through silence as sacred art we learn to appreciate silence as one significant dimension of an encounter with the sacred.

It is not an easy task to bring silence, art, and the sacred together. This is partly because we have so many differing interpretations of what constitutes deep silence, truly beautiful art, and transforming encounter with the sacred. More narrow and specific interpretations (for example, silence is just the absence of sound, art is only the fine arts, and the sacred is limited to the divine sphere) may limit our appreciation of how silence, art, and the sacred are truly part of our everyday living. We must choose to live in ways which bring out the best of silence, art, and the sacred in us and allow them to transform us. There is great value in this just as a human endeavor. There is even greater value in silence when it is a sacred art which deepens our relationship with the Divine One[3] and also each other.

Of course, when we aspire to encounter God, then silence (as a dimension of that encounter) is raised to being a sacred art in a different way from silence as a sacred art when, for example, we lift up in our arms for the first time a newborn baby. And so for us religious folks who seek God, it makes sense to reflect on, discover, and practice silence as a sacred art. In doing so we transcend our very selves. This is why bringing together silence, art, and the sacred is no easy task: we have the lofty desire to commune with God, entering into the very bliss of heaven.

First Consideration: Doing Art

Fresh out of college, I found myself substitute teaching at junior high school. My home room class included a particularly incorrigible group of youths—they were always into mischief and rather difficult for this untried teacher to control. Art class was a nightmare. Discipline? Forget it! Art class (when I strove to be faithful to the curriculum and the activities laid out for me in the teacher's guide) was a free for all! Besides, the rascals rejoined, they couldn't do art anyway ("We're not sissy artists; we're jocks!" was the retort of the boys). In desperation, I cast about for something which might catch their fancy. Finally, I hit upon calligraphy (probably because it's something I personally enjoy doing and was comfortable teaching it). With no money and few supplies, I had them begin simply by rubber banding together two pencils with the sharpened points at an angle, and showed them how to make flowing letters and shade them in. Well, lo and behold, the most obnoxious one among them became totally fascinated by the art of forming letters! At first, his were not particularly beautiful—hardly flowing and with different sizes and slants, he was all over the page. But, with practice, Mark's eye became trained and he made the most gorgeous Mother's Day card that spring. I think that was the proudest moment of his young life.

Those youths (and especially Mark) taught me something important: doing art is not necessarily reserved to professionals (except for the kind of art which comes up at Christie's in New York for auction), nor is doing art just another class in school which has little application and meaning for the nonprofessional beyond school. On the contrary; doing art is a human activity which many of us do in amazing ways when we break out of the mold of limited expectations. For example, some people are really doing art when they cook and present food; others do art when they lay out their flower beds in the spring and care for them through the growing season; still others do art when they listen to another during conversation and are able to bring out the best in the conversation partner.

Art is largely a matter of some activity catching one's fancy, focusing on doing it well, practicing and learning new forms and presentations, and then, of course, having something inside oneself to express. This sense of art is distinguished from art as *technē* (from the Greek, meaning "to practice a skill or trade"), undertaken by the "professional" artists. The "artists" to which we refer do not "make" in order to sell or trade; their livelihood does not depend upon it. But their good living does, as well as the quality of their life.

Mark taught me something else about art. Once he got interested in calligraphy, he became fixated on it—he drew letters during reading, math, English, geography, even during lunch hour. Art is something which we are *compelled* to

3

do when life wells up so large inside ourselves that we must express it somehow in all its symbolic power. The good cannot be contained, and art is our outlet for that which we experience deep within our selves. Whether we recognize it or not, art is an essential expression of who we are if we allow ourselves to feel deeply about anything at all.

My lesson in people and doing art is corroborated by no less a scholar than the ancient Greek philosopher Aristotle. In his *Nicomachean Ethics* (Book VI), Aristotle asserts that

> art is identical with a state of capacity [in the Greek, a "habit"] to make, involving a true sense of reasoning. All art is concerned with coming into being . . . and whose origin is in the maker and not in the thing made . . .[4]

Aristotle is saying that in art we *make*, and the making comes from within ourselves and is an expression of our very selves. Through art we ourselves come into being—we grow into a greater richness of who we are as a person. Art, then, isn't so much a choice about making some *thing*, as it is a choice about making *ourselves*, expressing ourselves, and *giving ourselves over* as gift to who or what is beyond ourselves. Art is the gift of ourselves to the world.

Commenting on Aristotle's "habit," French philosopher Jacques Maritain says that the habit of art is

> an inner quality or stable and deep-rooted disposition that raises the human subject and his [*sic*] natural powers to a higher degree of vital formation and energy—or that makes him possessed of a particular strength of his own: when a *habitus* . . . has developed in us, it becomes our most treasured good, our most unbending strength, because it is an ennoblement in the very kingdom of human nature and human dignity.[5]

Art, within this interpretation, is a habit which induces us to project ourselves in beautiful ways outside of ourselves. The very *doing* of art is ennobling—it enhances our dignity because it takes us outside of ourselves. Art enables us to share ourselves in unique and true ways with others. Lest we become stale and uninteresting, the habit of doing art energizes and enlivens us to strive beyond ourselves (yes, to transcend ourselves) so that we are ever fresh and new. The habit of art strengthens us to be more than we are. The habit of art most surely propels us toward the sacred, and silence is an essential and abiding feature of this habit.

From my viewpoint within the Judeo–Christian tradition, connecting doing art with personal dignity rests in the belief that we humans are made in God's image and likeness (see Genesis 1:26–27). God is the first and most expansive artist. The divine canvas began with nothing—"a formless void" and swirling waters. Onto this chaotic landscape the Divine Artist painted and sounded and chiseled and brought forth out of nothing the most beautiful work known—creation. And to crown it all, God created us humans not simply as one among many of God's creatures, but God created us in the divine image.

What might this astonishing assertion from Genesis mean—that we are made in the divine image? Beyond having intellect and will (the classical answer), I believe that we most image the Divine when, like the Divine, we are artists bringing forth out of our own beings our innermost precious selves. This is our dignity: to do as the Divine does and to share self with others. Our dignity (from the Latin *dignus,* meaning "worthy") is that we were created worthy to imitate our creator God by doing art.

All of us can appreciate the effort and fruit of truly gifted, professional artists. We enjoy the gorgeous visual art of painted landscapes, the pleasing sonorous art of a symphony, the proportion and balance of a beautifully designed building, the svelte of a well-choreographed ballet, the excellence of the art of well-crafted words in a pleasing poem. It is altogether too easy, however, to relegate all art to the singular achievements of a few. This narrow approach to the doing of art is surely unbecoming of our dignity as those created in the divine image. All of us are called to be artists if we wish to grow into our full potential as human beings created in the divine image. If we accept ourselves as artists and put on the habit of expressing ourselves as the Divine One sees us—as *very* good—then we have moved a giant step forward in more perfectly reflecting the image of the creator God. We have moved a giant step forward in reflecting who we are. Doing art draws us outside of ourselves and beyond ourselves into a domain of creative and creating self-expression, our unique donation of the beautiful to a world all too often mired in the ugly and banal. Moreover, doing art links us to others in a unique way by revealing ourselves in truth and goodness.

Reader Response Interlude

- To accept myself as an artist, I must . . .

- When by myself with a bit of time,
    I love to . . .

- This is what I do best . . . and know
    myself to be an artist in that . . .

- I have a sense of being "outside" and
    "beyond" myself when . . .

- I will try to . . .

Second Consideration: Seeking the Sacred

When I was a small child, walking into a Catholic church was an awe-inspiring experience. From my pint-size perspective, the building was as huge as the heavens themselves. Even when empty, in the silence the church still echoed loudly with the humble heartaches and joyful praises of generations who had gathered there. We were taught not to talk in church (nor would we have even thought it—the building and people mediated something which caught our attention), and we knew in church we stepped into the presence of God and touched the sacred. When the building filled with people waiting patiently for the service to begin, there was still deep, echoing silence. Somehow even the coughing and fidgeting of the multitudinous assembly settled into a cocoon of peace and expectation. Not even a multi-voiced choir or majestic pipe organ could smother the beckoning silence. Silence and sound together knit us into one heart and voice. There was real art to this rhythm—a conscious making of something beautiful from the silence and sound of being together for the common purpose of worship. We knew something sacred was about to happen. Rather than seeking the sacred, it sought us. As a child I wasn't always conscious of the sacred while in church; admittedly, my mind was often elsewhere during the services. But over the years the silence formed me and nourished me nonetheless.

Thinking of the sacred naturally turns our thoughts to religious places, holy people, and God-filled experiences. Even so, this is hardly our only experience of the sacred and sometimes not even our most profound. Consider the thundering silence which pierces us between the notes of taps being played at a military funeral when a lifetime of service and sacrifice is packed into this flickering, intervening time. This, too, is an encounter with the sacred. Or another common, communal experience: what is it that we do when we observe a moment of silence in memory of someone or some event, for example, when on September 11 we pause midmorning to remember what happened in New York City, Pennsylvania, and Washington, DC? What happens during those slow moments of the changing of the guard at the Tomb of the Unknowns in Arlington National Cemetery? Carried far beyond a person or event, these moments of collective and silent encounter with the sacred give relief to grief (or expression to joy) and enkindle resolve and courage. We seek these moments because only in the silence do we salve and savor our unleashed emotion. Thus, there are two kinds of sacred: the Sacred *which seeks us* in divine encounter and the sacred *we ourselves seek* in powerful times of collective memory.

The word *sacred* comes from the Latin *sacer* and, as with most words, consulting a Latin dictionary opens up numerous possibilities. "Sacred" refers to the holy or to that which is consecrated and dedicated; further, "holy" refers to the pure, virtuous, blameless. Two worlds open up here. First, we hold sacred that to which we are committed (consecrated, dedicated), that in which we have a stake, that which motivates us to single-mindedness in thought or purpose. Second, we hold sacred that which we perceive as wholesome and innocent (pure, virtuous, blameless). The two worlds clearly are mutually engaging. Although we might be single-minded about something which is harmful to us (for example, any addiction), in general we consider sacred that which is both absorbing and beneficial, unique and good.

All of us have our "sacred cows." For some, it might be Sunday football (or basketball or golf). For others it might be Saturday shopping. For still others it might be singing happy birthday even when no one can hold a tune. Most of us have family traditions which we hold sacred, even in this age of the lament of the breakdown of the family (let alone of the extended family). We might grab meals on the run most of the time, but when it comes to the big holidays or holy days (for example, Thanksgiving, Christmas, Passover, Fourth of July, Fast-Breaking at the end of Ramadan), we have a natural sense that for the celebration to be full we must join with others outside our immediate family in order to make the festivities fuller. Perhaps this is why we miss departed loved ones at these times—we've always had grandma and grandpa over at Thanksgiving, and now there is an emptiness because a comfortable and expected tradition must take on new parameters.

We also use sacred in other everyday contexts (sometimes using the language "thus and so is sacrosanct"). We sometimes joke that the harried parent only has one sacred place—the bathroom. We hold values sacred—as citizens of a democracy, we defend our right to life, liberty, and the pursuit of happiness; our right to free speech; our right to self-govern. We hold actions as sacred—a kiss, for example; and if a kiss is insincere, we feel betrayed; no wonder for us Christians Judas' kiss is a particularly poignant way for Judas to give a betraying sign of identity (see Matthew 26:48). We hold words as sacred—one's name, for example, which is so intimately connected with self, with who one is. No wonder we get upset when someone calls us by another name or by a derisive name.

In all these instances of experiencing the sacred, we are drawn to that in which we have a stake, that which makes a difference for us. The sacred both focuses us, rallies us, and gives us insight into a new world of possibilities. A story illustrates this.

When I was in the lower grades in elementary school, I didn't like my name. I wanted to be "Nancy," the most popular name at that time. It was only years later when my mother and I were reminiscing one day that I heard how I got to be named Joyce. I was born while my father was overseas, near the end of World War II. In fact, I was born about a month before peace was signed with Germany. Mother said she knew then that the end was near and that Dad was safe and would come home. So she named me "Joyce" because she was so overjoyed at Dad's imminent return. From that moment onward, my name became very sacred to me. I perceived myself in a whole new way, and became aware that my very existence bundled up for my mother the grief of separation, the horrors and mortal dangers of war, and the overwhelming joy of reunion and safety. With the revelation of this sacred story, I became a different person, and this new self-perception opened up new possibilities for how I would choose to live each day. I was particularly confirmed of this new self-awareness one day around my birthday when I paid the bill at a restaurant after Sunday brunch. Taking my change and thanking the cashier, she looked at me and said, "You have a beautiful smile." I didn't take the time to tell her the real origin of my smile: the joy of who I am and how I came to be named.

Now let us approach the sacred from a different perspective. Here, the sacred "is an absolute reality . . . which transcends this world but manifests itself in this world, thereby sanctifying it and making it real."[6] For historian of religion Mircea Eliade, the sacred is a "mode of being."[7] By describing the sacred in this way, we are able to go beyond the sacred as something we hold dear (although we do that as well), to something beyond ourselves, which transcends ourselves. This takes us to the world of mystery and spirit.

An aphorism which has been circulating for a long time is that "a mystery is not a problem to be solved but a life to be lived." To a strictly scientific mind set, everything unknown can be approached as a problem—given enough time and research, we can find the answer. Problems are hurdles to be overcome. This attitude actually works often in our favor and is important for dealing well with many aspects of our lives. For example, we all await the day when we will have cracked the problem of how to cure cancer or AIDS.

Other aspects of our lives, however, are diminished if we treat them as mere problems to be solved. For example, if an engaged couple approaches getting to know each other as a problem, the marriage is in trouble before the vows are ever exchanged. Knowledge of the other simply as a problem implies that eventually one can know everything there is to know about the other. This simply leaves open the door to confine, control, abuse the other—or at least to get bored with the other. On the other hand, if we approach the other as a mystery, there is always room to discover new things about the other and we know the other can never be exhausted. No matter how long a couple lives together, there will always be something new and fresh to discover about the other. Perhaps one reason a couple married for fifty or more years begins to act alike and sometimes even look alike is that they have appropriated to themselves their knowledge of each other and made it their own, but have become unattached to the knowledge itself (and so are unaware of how alike they are) as they look for ever new discoveries.

Mystery always contains a richness and depth which can never be exhausted. The "inexhaustibleness" of mystery is what transcends us, what we call sacred, and what transports us into the world of spirit. Today there is renewed interest in spirituality (a way to live by a set of values or norms), and for good reason. In a society where so many of us have so much, we long for that which we cannot easily purchase or have. We long for that which we do not control, but for what is of inestimable value which instead helps us blossom as persons.

Spirituality always requires something of us—its cost is nothing less than *kenosis* (the discipline of self-emptying). Here is where sacred, art, and silence all come together. In *kenosis* we form the habit of projecting ourselves into the beauty of self-transcendence, and by doing so stand not only in silent awe before our selves, but also before the world in which we live. In *kenosis* the deepest sense of who we are becomes at hand in the stark reality of at-handness, available for anyone who dares to stop and see. We are who we are. Even with our imperfections and foibles, the human being is a work of art, one who shares in the sacred.

Finally, let's speak of the sacred specifically in terms of the divine. Now the mode of being of the sacred is manifested in the utter transcendence and absoluteness of the divine creator God. While we use the words *transcendence* and *absoluteness* to refer to God, the remarkable thing about our God is that the Divine One is still immanent, always desiring to relate to us, to teach us virtue and good living, to coax us into the faith and hope which draws us out of ourselves toward eternity itself. It is precisely the play between divine transcendence and imminence which spurs our desire to encounter the sacred.

The Hebrew word for the presence of God is *shekinah* and usually refers to God's presence in the Temple, but God's presence is sometimes very at hand for humans. Moses experienced it in a burning bush. Isaiah had a vision of "the Lord sitting on a throne, high and lofty" and exclaimed that he is a sinful, doomed man, for "my eyes have seen the King, the LORD of hosts!" (Isaiah 6:1, 5); in the presence of the Divine, Isaiah is cleansed and receives his prophetic mission. Peter, James, and John experienced Jesus' appearance at the transfiguration changing to "dazzling white" who "appeared in glory" (Luke 9:29, 31). The glory and majesty of God for believers is so desirous that we seek the sacred presence precisely in order to transcend ourselves. When we lose ourselves in the sacred, we become more than ourselves.

The call of every believer is to be a mystic, one initiated into the *shekinah* of God. As Hugo Rahner proposes, "The . . . mystic . . . is one who sees through visible things and perceives the inexpressible that lies beyond."[8] The mystic, therefore, is one who is practiced in recognizing God's theophanies (God's self-revelation, which is more at hand than we sometimes like to admit) and moves beyond the at-hand to the power and potential revealed. Any experience of the sacred is essentially a mystical moment.

The Judeo–Christian, Muslim, and other religious traditions all have their share of recognized mystics. As interest in spirituality has grown, so has interest in the classical mystics. Feminists have made household names out of Julian of Norwich and Hildegaard of Bingen. Scant attention has been paid, however, to how every seeker of the sacred is truly a mystic.

The mystic, through contemplation and *kenosis*, surrenders self to the mystery of divine love, mercy, and goodness; and in losing (surrendering) self, finds a new self. Unlike the great mystics of the world religions, our own mysticism is more fleeting, less predictable, and (usually) less intense. This makes these experiences, however, no less mystical.

All of us at times have known deep within ourselves an immediate experience of God which left us in awe, joy, and wonder. Seeking the sacred encourages us to pause long enough to recognize these experiences as a gift of intimate Divine Presence. Frequently we recognize mystical moments at emotionally charged times: being washed with comfort during intense grief at the death of a loved one, having an overwhelming sense of peace in the midst of a family crisis, hearts leaping with joy at the sight of a spectacular sunrise or sunset. More challenging is to recognize mystical moments—an overwhelming sense of God's presence—even during the simple routine of our everyday lives.

No matter what our approach to or understanding of the sacred is, there is always an absoluteness and transcendence about it because we know it exists apart from ourselves and is pure gift. Surrendering ourselves, the sacred possesses us and opens us to heretofore unimaginable riches. The sacred takes what God created as *very good*, and makes it even better.

Reader Response Interlude

- Examples of daily sacred moments for me are . . .

- I am aware of myself as a sacred person when . . .

- My mystical experiences of the Divine Presence have taught me . . .

Putting It All Together: Why Silence Is a Sacred Art

When I am in my office doing routine work that doesn't require creativity or concerted concentration, I often have a stereo tuned softly to the local classical station. I appreciate my local public radio station because it seldom has chatter—no commercials, little commentary, very short news briefs. Mostly, the station offers just the music. Years ago when I became personally attuned to a weekly rhythm of fasting on Friday (for Christians, the day of the cross) and feasting on Sunday (the day to celebrate the joy and glory of the Resurrection[9]), I began to turn off my radio on Fridays in preparation for and anticipation of Sunday. The silence speaks to me so well of how Friday differs from other days. I find myself often looking forward to this particular day of silence and the unique solitude it brings. I've often thought of perhaps having more days with no music. But then the rhythm would be destroyed. There is an art to this rhythm—a conscious making of beauty from within the absence of music which creates the sheer silence. With respect to beauty and silence, Max Picard has this to say:

> Beauty is also present in silence; it is primarily in silence. Silence would sink weighted down into its own darkness, down to the abyss, dragging down with it much that belongs to the brightness of earth, if beauty were not also present in silence. Beauty gives a lightness and airiness to silence so that it, too, becomes a part of the brightness of earth. Beauty relieves silence of its heaviness, brings it up into the light of earth and brings it to man. The radiance of the beauty which rests on silence is a premonition of the radiance inhering in the word of truth.[10]

Silence can only be a sacred art when we make a daily habit of sustaining the truth of its life-giving beauty and peace. Habits come about only when we value a practice and then do it over and over again until the practice is truly a part of the fabric of our very being. When we are convinced of the value and truth of silence as a sacred art, we make time even in our busy lives to seek it, treasure it, expect it. What fosters the habit of silence and encourages us to cultivate it is the good which comes out of the silent moments we create. Silence becomes sacred art when we teach ourselves to fashion out of it the beauty which is a touch of Divine Presence and which transforms us into more than we are. We need silence lest we become stagnant and miss the pervading desire for growth, bringing us to a share in *shekinah*. We need silence so that we can stand with Moses on holy ground.

When we speak of silence as a sacred art, we are intimating that all silence has the potential for ultimate value, can take us to Divine Presence, and can bring us to more than we are. Much is at stake in the practice of silence. Silence keeps our lives from becoming routine and boring, opens us to mystery, and is the medium out of which our most worthwhile relationships grow. Yes, so much more is at stake when we approach and embrace silence as sacred art.

- Silence is sacred art when it is the medium out of which we (and God) purposefully fashion ever more finely the beauty of ourselves, becoming more perfectly the creation God intends us to be.

- Silence is sacred art when it forms within us the habit of opening ourselves to all the wonder of everything at hand and which can carry us beyond ourselves to new possibilities, new modes of existence, ever new choices which re-create us, delight us, and nurture us.

- Silence is sacred art when it salves our pain, deepens our joy, and redirects us to seek more than we are and do.

- Silence is sacred art when it beckons us to bring peace to our own little corner of the world (thus, bringing the hope of peace to the whole world), to act justly toward others, to be satisfied with less so others can have what they need.

- Silence is sacred art when it increases our capacity to see the sublime in the mundane, majesty in the ordinary, and goodness even in what is fractured.

- Silence is sacred art when it enables us to forget ourselves and redirect our attention and affection toward others and their good.

- Silence is sacred art when it rekindles our energy to do good and lifts our spirit so that we can breathe new life into our everyday activities.

- Silence is sacred art when it fosters new ideas from seemingly nowhere, new resolves from the hopelessness of discouragement, new hope from the darkness of aimlessness and boredom.

- Silence is sacred art when it energizes us to forgive because our own integrity calls ourselves and others to name our mistakes for what they are—just mistakes. Silence helps us realize that mistakes do not diminish who we are but are opportunities to become more wise. Silence helps us realize that even our sinfulness is an opportunity to open ourselves to God's mercy and grow in holiness.

- Silence is sacred art when it gets us so in touch with ourselves that we are better able to be present to others, especially those who are near and dear. Silence helps us avoid taking others for granted. It warns us not to use others for our own selfish gains.

- Silence is sacred art when it causes the realization of how gifted we truly are to well up within ourselves. Only in silence, when we brush away things and cares, can we become so very aware of the richness we possess. This has nothing to do with possessions and everything to do with the endless imagination of all that is good and true and beautiful.

- Silence is sacred art when it brings us to bow down in self-actualizing humility before the beauty of a God who loves us more than we can imagine or appreciate.

- Silence is sacred art when it is the interval from frenetic lives to fantastic calm, re-creating us in ever new ways.

NOTES

1. Thomas L. Friedman, *From Beirut to Jerusalem* (New York: Anchor Books, A Division of Random House, Inc., 1990) 75.

2. The author's choice of language about God makes this work more accessible to readers from other faith traditions.

3. I use the word *moment* here not as a chronological period which can be counted in seconds or mnutes, but as a point in time filled with meaning. We might profitably contrast here the two Greek words referring to time: *chronos* means "counting time"; *kairos* means "a point in time pregnant with meaning," which might last but a blink of an eye, or a minute or hour or day or even week. Duration isn't important with *kairos*, but what happens in the moment is significant.

4. Aristotle, *What Is Art?* trans. W. D. Ross in *Philosophies of Art and Beauty: Selected Readings in Aesthetics from Plato to Heidegger*, eds. Albert Hofstadter and Richard Kuhn (New York: The Modern Library, 1964) 83.

5. Jacques Maritain, *Creative Intuition in Art and Poetry: The A. W. Mellon Lectures in the Fine Arts* (Cleveland and New York: Meridian Books, The World Publishing Company, 1953) 35.

6. Mircea Eliade, *The Sacred and the Profane: The Nature of Religion*, trans. Willard R. Trask (New York: Harcourt, Brace & World, Inc., A Harvest Book, 1959) 202.

7. See, for example, pp. 12, 14–16, 202 in *Eliade, The Sacred and the Profane*. Eliade describes two modes of being, the sacred and the profane, and they are opposites.

8. Hugo Rahner, *Man at Play*, pref. Walter J. Ong, trans. Brian Battershaw and Edward Quinn (New York: Herder and Herder, 1972) 54.

9. Most other religious traditions experience a parallel weekly rhythm. For example, Jews might experience a rhythm between Friday as a day of Sabbath preparation and Saturday as the Sabbath; Muslims might experience a rhythm between noon prayer on other days of the week and the required Friday communal prayer in the mosque.

10. Max Picard, *The World of Silence*, pref. Gabriel Marcel, trans. Stanley Godwin (Wichita, Kansas: Eighty Day Press, 2002 [originally published in English by Regnery Gateway, 1952]) 34.

PART ONE

Silence and Everyday Living

CHAPTER 2

From Frenetic Lives to Fantastic Calm

It is said today that people need only go into the country to reach the "quietness of nature" and silence. But they do not meet the silence there; on the contrary, they carry the noise of the great towns and the noise of their own souls out into the country with them.[1]

Being comfortable with silence is toilsome and illusive for many. After all, we have become so accustomed to sound-noises—every minute seems to be filled with its pervasiveness. We contend with traffic and machinery; empty chatter and uproarious laughter; with TV, radio, and stereos; doorbells and telephones; dryer, microwave, and oven bells; factory whistles and the stamp of a time clock; and the always-so-jarring sound of an alarm clock. We live in a never-ceasing pandemonium of sounds which crowd our attention and constantly distract us.

Oh, yes, we could build ourselves a sound-proof cocoon and escape from all this sound. Yes, we could go to the "quietness of nature" and pretend that the sound isn't there. Nevertheless, even then we would not enjoy the grace of life-filled silence. Pretending to silence only takes our sound-noises with us. In addition to sound-noises, we also must consider what might be termed "personal silence."

Personal silence is the practice of profoundly stilling our bodies and focusing our minds and easing our spirits. This kind of stillness can take place in the middle of New York's Grand Central Station or in downtown *Our Town*. It takes but a fleeting moment of our time. Personal silence is the disciplined luxury of single-mindedness, single-heartedness, and deep spirituality. It is attentiveness to self and others and—yes, most importantly—attentiveness to the Other who reveals the Divine Self to us so intimately and compassionately. Personal silence can calm our nerves or help us focus our attention; it allows silence to be with us wherever we are, be that in the bustle of everyday life or in the quiet of nature. But most importantly, personal silence enables us to become aware of God's abiding and gracious presence to us.

In the next chapter we consider more closely all that goes into personal silence: quieting noise, stilling the body, focusing the mind, calming the spirit. Before we move to an extended reflection on personal silence itself, however, it is good to pause to look at the freneticism of our lives which binds and surrounds us. We want to look beyond the frenetic pace of our lives to a beckoning fantastic calm which frees and enfolds us.

From Frenetic Lives

When one of my nieces was in high school, she described an average after-school time for her: school swim team practice, class officer meeting, city league soccer game, chemistry lab study group, cell phone chatting with her friends, homework. Six activities, and eventually she did manage to catch some sleep. I think sometime in the late afternoon and evening was supper (no doubt fast food grabbed on the run). I'm certain nowhere during that time was there silence or rest or simply time to regroup, as she chased from one activity to the next. Now, my niece is a fine young lady: she was in the honor society, faithfully did her share of the work around the house, was active in her church, always took time to write thank you notes after Christmas and her birthday. As I listened to her talk about her life, I clearly could detect energy and enthusiasm. Furthermore, she is a thoughtful young woman, tending to think through decisions carefully, and generally not one to waste time or talent. She's older now—graduated with honors from college and working, still seemingly keeping as frenetic a pace as in high school. I wonder: for how long? When will it catch up with her?

Most of us live lives which are way too busy, filled with way too many different kinds of activities, with way too much of it ultimately pointless. We fill every waking minute with something or someone. It is as though we are afraid to be alone—afraid of loneliness or being left behind. Worse still, some of us simply fall into this kind of frenzied life by default, rarely stopping long enough to evaluate what we do and why we do it. Sometimes we become aware of being utterly exhausted—even the young and fresh among us often look tired and worn out. But rarely do we take the time to take stock of what we are doing and why.

Some people have no actual choice about their tremendous busy-ness. We've all met the single parent, for example, who is working two full-time jobs at not much above minimum wage, barely eking out enough subsistence to house, feed, and clothe the family. We've listened to this parent cry pitifully that there is not enough time left to give the children the attention, discipline, and direction they need to make something of themselves and break out of the cycle of poverty. Or we've met the elderly spouse who is taking care of an Alzheimer-stricken loved one, dog tired with the constant care, and yet complains little that there is no time for self because love somehow eases the weariness and gives strength and courage.

What is amazing about these and other kinds of frenetic life situations is that in spite of no minutes to spare and bone tiredness, there is usually a kind of peace and calm within the individual—a tranquility which comes from willing self-giving for the sake of another.

There are many, many self-giving and generous people living and working among us. They daily do extraordinary things for the good of others. For a long time after the late summer anniversary of Hurricane Katrina, we saw documentaries on TV about the heroic efforts perfect strangers put out to save and help others, sometimes going days without sleep (this is also true for other national disasters elsewhere). The frenetic pace of this service brings bone tiredness, but it also includes peace and deep joy at the connection to others the volunteer service brings. Frenetic activity and heroic responses aren't always at the cost of peace and tranquility. Often they enhance it in the long run. These kinds of activities are always purposeful and take us out of ourselves toward others. Our lives are seldom without activity. Activity isn't the issue; purposefulness, generosity, other-centeredness, and ultimate goals are the issues which must be considered if our lives are not simply frenetic.

Another kind of frenetic activity, however, precipitates only unrest, irritation, and sometimes anger. Here we not only fill up every moment of our waking hours with relentless doing, but all too often there is minimal reason for what we are doing. The proverbial couch potato who sits in front of the TV five or more hours in an evening is actually engaged in frenetic activity, even though on the surface the person is doing nothing. Frenetic activity, then, is not determined simply by constant doing, but also by non-doing which is merely a matter of filling up time with little or no personal growth or betterment. Avoiding responsibility might also be a kind of frenetic activity, as are conversation-monopolizing chatter (especially if it's about oneself) and compulsive behaviors.

Frenetic activity is the enemy of silence because it robs us of the self-discipline necessary to focus on a single task at hand or to be attentive to who and what surrounds us. This kind of purposeless activity scatters us. It keeps us unconnected. It causes us to lose our center. It leaves us exhausted but not able to rest. We may accomplish much, but are seldom energized. This kind of frenetic activity causes us to lose our center and lose sight of who we are and what life is truly all about. This kind of frenetic activity scatters us rather than centers us; it drains us rather than fulfills us. In the end, this kind of frenetic activity robs us of who we are.

It takes a great deal of resolve to get a handle on the needless activity in our daily lives and redirect our energy to something more lasting. One step forward is to decide what is essential activity and what we take on for no better reason than that something is there before us to do. Assessing the pace of our frenetic activity leads us to prioritize where and how we want to spend our time. Time is precious; we only have so much of it. It is always a challenge to use our time well to the purposes which ultimately count.

Any reflection on frenetic activity must raise the issue of our relationship to goods and services. It's one thing to work two shifts because we have hungry children, must pay the rent, have medical expenses, and never seem to have enough income to take care of necessities. It's quite another to work eighty-hour weeks because we want bigger houses, the latest SUV, and every new gadget on the market. There is nothing wrong in itself with having things. When things, however, become the center of our life and existence, then it is time to evaluate our priorities and examine the expenditure of energy involved with our frenetic activites. Sometimes quietness and relaxation come in most unexpected places at most unexpected time. I learned this myself only through experience.

One choice I make about how I spend my leisure time has taught me a great deal. A long time ago I developed a habit of spending some time most Sunday afternoons visiting a retirement center near me because of relatives who are residents there. At first, I only spent time with the people I know and whom I came to visit. But gradually over time, I began to know other residents by name. A brief smile and hello soon became unsatisfactory and I would stop and exchange some pleasantries for a few minutes. Often I would hear the same stories over and over again. When I would get ready to leave my house (especially on a cold winter afternoon), I would sometimes think to myself that I would rather just stay home and use the time for myself. What has fascinated me over the years is not so much my commitment to and respect for the elderly (I was taught that as a very young child) as the dawning realization that these visits have become a necessary part of my habit of silence. Encounters with the elderly are most often occasions for listening. I have learned that instead of being worried about spending my time doing something which I consider productive, these visits are actually precious moments of leisure and silence. They are moments when I am taking in far more than I am giving. They are a guarantee that for at least a part of one day some of my time is not spent in frenetic activity, but is spent in quiet presence. These visits have reminded me of what is most precious in my life—the people I love and my desire that they have the best quality of life possible.

Reader Response Interlude

- On an average day, my frenetic activities are . . .

- I am able to halt frenetic activity when . . .

- My priorities are . . .

- These are what is getting in the way of my putting aside frenetic activity . . .

- I need to . . .

To Fantastic Calm

The English word *fantastic* conjures up in us notions of preposterous, surreal, over the edge. It seems an unlikely word to choose as the opposite of frenetic and a goal toward which our silence might take us. Without totally losing this appeal to the outlandish and unthinkable (especially when we think of our boldness about the Divine), we also can consider *fantastic* from its root in the Greek verb *phantazein* which means "to make visible" or "to appear." Images and imagination are one way we engage a world which is more than material. Images and imagination unleash the spirit within us and release the freedom of our own being. Philosopher Suzanne Langer writes that

> Image-making is, then, the mode of our untutored thinking, and stories are its earliest product. We think of things happening, remembered or imaginary or prospective; we see with the mind's eye . . . Pictures and stories are the mind's stock-in-trade. Those larger, more complex elements that symbolize events may contain more than merely visual ingredients, kinesthetic and aural and perhaps yet other factors, wherefore it is misleading to call them "story-images"; I will refer to them as "fantasies."[2]

Fantasies and imagination are a healthy way for us to make visible our deepest yearnings. Not all fantasies, then, are unreal or unconnected with the everyday world in which we live. Fantasies (mind pictures and stories) enable us to "see" deceased loved ones, remember formidable and formational events, re-create in order to learn from past behaviors and relationships.

Langer, in her use of "untutored thinking," nudges us into reflecting on another aspect of images and imagination. Most of our speech and activity is necessarily controlled. We desire to say and do the right thing because this facilitates good relationships and breeds harmony. We do things right because that is how good products are produced, good transactions are completed, good reputations are built.

Another set of words for *fantasy* might be *untutored thinking*. Fantasy—especially in the free play of aloneness—presses for a safe release of self and an expression of creativity in which we need not worry about producing something worthy and under the scrutinizing eye of others. Thus, fantasy is the friend of freedom.

How many of the stories of the Nazi concentration camps include larger-than-life examples of prisoners who, despite near starvation, constant fear, and torture, nevertheless never lost hope and even produced marvelous pieces of art in various forms. Dietrich Bonhoeffer's *Letters and Papers from Prison* (published posthumously) is but one particular example. More than simple day-to-day telling of events, the book evidences creative theological thinking in the most trying of times and conditions. How did so many never lose hope? Surely for most prisoners their faith provided them with strength and an abiding presence of God. At the same time, although the soldiers could deprive them of almost everything which makes one human, no one could take from these beautiful souls their imaginations—their inward freedom and God-given ability to imagine alternative and better times and places. No one could take from them the gifts of being created in the image of God—the gift to create out of nothing. In their imaginations and shared stories, loved ones were still present and some modicum of the "good life" could still be had.

The Nazis could lock up people in their concentration camps, but they could not steal from those whom they made barely alive the utter aliveness of their undaunted spirits. Isn't it ironic that the inscription over the gates of the prison camps reads even to this day, *Arbeit mach Frei* (Work makes free)? I remember being particularly struck by this as I stood in reverence before the main gate of Dachau in southern Germany. I thought when I first saw the inscription over the gate that perhaps the prison keepers had in mind an encouragement to the people passing through the gates—that if they cooperated and worked hard enough they would go free (my knowledge of history prodded me with the stark reality that this was not the case). In fact, as I walked through the camp (in utter, utter silence; it seemed a desecration to speak in anything but a whisper, if at all), I became so very aware of a different meaning. In no way could the barbed wire and hard labor of the camps entomb the faith and imagination of the prisoners. They were caged, yet magnificently free. Because their spirit could not be killed.

Suzanne Langer can help us grasp at least a bit of what happened in those concentration camps. She makes the claim that

> . . . with their realistic presence, the imaginative process is carried over from dream to reality; fantasy is externalized in the veneration of "sacra." . . . The power of conception—of having "ideas"—is man's [*sic*] peculiar asset, and awareness of this power is an exciting sense of human strength. Nothing is more thrilling than the dawn of a new conception. The symbols that embody basic ideas . . . are naturally sacred . . . . Such notions rest on a natural identification of symbolic values with practical values, of the expressive with the physical functions of a thing. . . . The contemplation of sacra invites a certain intellectual excitement— intellectual because it centers in a mental activity—the excitement of *realizing* life and strength, manhood, context, and death. The whole cycle of human emotions is touched by such a contemplation.[3]

In this marvelous passage we have an explicit link of imagination, contemplation, the sacred, freedom, and fantastic calm. More than "intellectual excitement," imagination which brings visibility or appearance (*phantazein*) often brings even physical excitement, and in that a convincing amount of energy is released.

No doubt the memory of the countless deaths (and even a lingering scent) brought me to my silent knees at Dachau. At the same time I had another equally strong memory: of the creative and productive imagination-spirit of those who had been entombed there. This evoked in me sacred awe as much as the deaths. From the recesses of one's own spirit comes life, not death—even long after the camps have been closed. The cloistered convent on the grounds stands as a living memorial of the silent spirit-creativity which took place there over a half century ago.

Closely associated with imagination and freedom is the activity of play. No where does play or leisure present itself more aptly as the enjoyment of freedom as in the play of children. Here both the unstructured and the structured meet head on in a glorious dance of abandon and freedom. In play a child's imagination runs free, constructing whole worlds in which the child shapes reality. It's interesting to compare toys of today with those of yesteryear. Toys once were simple, often homemade. They were much more suggestive, and so nurtured the imagination. Now many, if not most, of children's toys are so ready-packaged that there is little left to the imagination, especially in terms of how the children might imitate the adult world.

Many of us have experienced a small child opening a gift at holidays or birthday (especially one in a very large box), only to find the child more fascinated with the wrapping paper, ribbon, and box than with the gift inside. It's also true that if a number of gifts are piled up for the child, he or she will go for the largest one first. No matter that perhaps the four foot box has a paper kite in it worth a couple of dollars while perhaps a six-inch-square box has a much more expensive electronic game. For the child and imagination, large is good. It's the imagination which sets free the secrets of the paper and ribbon and box—and so, yes, large is good. Often observers can actually see the little minds working as they construct their play, first in utter silence as they work out the simple particulars, and then in joy as they live in their comfortable fantasy.

My brother has about three quarters of an acre for a side yard. When his children were all home yet and still in elementary school, that yard was a magnet, serving as the gathering place for the neighborhood children. Sometimes there could be fifteen or so youngsters playing together, of all ages and sizes and shapes. Often the numbers prompted a baseball game. Now, we all know baseball has pretty standard rules. However, it was always fascinating for me to watch these children at play. The older ones were quite willing to make room for the younger ones. They also were quite adept at setting aside the standard rules of the game and making up and agreeing upon rules which better worked for them. When the little ones came up to bat, they were allowed six strikes. If the ball was hit, never mind that the four-year-old batter would run and pick it up and carry it to first base—that way no one could tag the rascal out. The little ones were always safe. Sometimes one would run straight from first to third. The tolerance of their rule-making was amazing. In the companionship of their neighborhood group, they adjusted rules to fit their needs. And the whole play was about having fun and respecting and caring for each other.

So much of children's free time today is organized by adults into what are really adult activities. We make the rules for them, and sometimes we can be quite harsh when the children don't keep them well or live up to our expectations. Too often sports or dancing lessons or other kinds of "leisure" activities are so demanding and stressful that they are counter-productive in terms of how play helps form children into spiritual, emotional, psychological, and socially healthy adults. When we over-program children's play, we steal from them opportunities to imagine and play in their own world, where they are comfortable and success-ful and safe.

On occasion, during some unguarded moments, we adults sometimes also give ourselves over to the sheer reverie of genuine play. When out for an evening's walk and coming upon a child's hopscotch game crudely chalked on the sidewalk, how many of us don't skip along the number blocks? For those few seconds we are children again, with all the abandon and imagination which re-creates us into the greening of life. It's wonderful that porch rockers and swings are popular again. A leisurely evening quietly rocking or swinging, listening to the sounds of nature, smelling the fragrance of new-mown grass and flowers, beholding the glory of a summer sunset refreshes us in a way that TV or video games cannot.

Giving ourselves permission regularly to take sufficient time to allow the fantastic with its calm to break in on us brings us face to face with our own inner spirit. Giving sufficient time in silence for us to become acquainted with what is becoming visible or appearing to us is a way for us to discover new things about ourselves and discard old things which are burdensome. This silent time helps us discover new things in and about the world in which we live. The fantastic sets us free precisely because it is something out of the ordinary erasing expectations and predictable responses. Embracing the fantastic is to dispense with control and enter into fresh calm. It is to unleash our spirit so that God's Holy Spirit might re-create us.

Reader Response Interlude

- The frenetic rears up in my life when . . . It kills my spirit when . . .

- The unstructured dance of my own imagination is . . .

- I feel most free when . . .

- I enjoy the imagination and freedom of play when I . . .

- I delight in the fantastic when . . .

- I experience a fantastic calm most often when . . .

How to Go from Frenetic Lives to Fantastic Calm

We live in a fast-paced world. Electronics have shrunk the world so that everyone else's business is also our own business. We can no longer be isolated; what happens across the world affects us here in "our town." With the demands of family, work, church, civic duties, we are all caught up in a frenetic pace of living. Silence is the red light which forces us to stop. Silence is the bridge between our frenetic everyday living and the rest and vitality of fantastic calm. In the imagination and freedom of the fantastic, we ourselves are unleashed.

It's relatively easy to move from a frenetic pace of life to a fantastic engagement with reality. All we need do is re-evaluate our priorities and decide that we can probably settle for a lot less in life and end up much happier. We can decide to commit ourselves to time each day to allow ourselves the freedom to imagine, to create, to spend our time with quality. Perhaps the biggest challenge in moving from the frenetic living to fantastic calm is evaluating our leisure time and asking ourselves if the time does truly re-create us. Our leisure cannot be about *doing*, but must be about *being*.

We have really been reflecting on and building a case for the value of silence. Now we are ready to consider more specifically the meaning of silence itself in its many dimensions. This is the undertaking of the next chapter.

NOTES

1. Max Picard, *The World of Silence*, pref. Gabriel Marcel, trans. Stanley Godwin (Wichita, Kansas: Eighty Day Press, 2002 [originally published in English by Regnery Gateway, 1952]) 132.

2. Suzanne K. Langer, *Philosophy in a New Key: A Study in the Symbolism of Reason, Rite, and Art* (New York and Toronto: The New American Library, Inc., A Mentor Book, 1942, 1951) 128.

3. Langer, *Philosophy in a New Key*, 132–33; italics in original.

CHAPTER 3

Living Silence with Comfort and Ease

Twofold is the meaning of silence. One, the abstinence from speech, the absence of sound. Two, inner silence, the absence of self-concern, stillness. One may articulate words in his voice and yet be inwardly silent. One may abstain from uttering any sound and yet be overbearing.[1]

Where I live evening darkness begins to come noticeably earlier around the beginning of October. And with this darkness comes a certain mood: day is ending, work is (supposedly) completed, quiet settles upon us. Quiet . . . stillness . . . silence . . . even the cycle of nature draws us into a rhythm of quiet and stillness, affords us the luxury of slowing down to learn once again how to appreciate silence. Nature, further, invites us even to more: its rhythm is already forming a habit of silence in which we re-evaluate who we are and what we most desire out of our fragile lives.

We say again: silence is something of which we seem to have so very little. Moreover, quality silence is more than simply an absence of sound-noise; true, deep silence absorbs every part of our selves, both external and internal. Silence requires the stilling of sound-noise, but it also requires body stillness, mind stillness, and soul stillness. True, deep silence absorbs our whole being.

The great Jewish mystic Abraham Heschel recognized that it is not sufficient to think of silence as the absence of sound. In this chapter, we expand Heschel's suggestion that the meaning of silence is twofold (outer and inner) into a fourfold consideration—outer silence which includes noise and body stillness, and inner silence which includes mind and soul stillness. Rather than define silence (which really defies tacking it down in any way that its mystery and art are limited), we seek here to describe it and also perhaps experience it in all its richness.

A Detour: The Negative Side of Silence

Before going any further, we must make a slight but important detour, and point out that the whole thrust of these pages is to explore the positive value of silence for one's life. When we speak of silence as a habit, we are assuming that this is a *good* habit. Admittedly, silence has a negative side and can be used in harmful and hurtful ways.

For example, someone can go into a fruitless silence which does nothing else than shut out the world and others. We might speak of getting a "cold shoulder" from someone—the body language is clear here (stay away!). This is an example of a harmful use of silence. Another example: sometimes silence can be a way for someone to be in denial. If we give some helpful suggestions to another (this could be anything from self-improvement nudges to a better idea about how to accomplish a work task) and the suggestions are met with silence, this might be an indication that the receiving individual is in denial about needing help or change.

Sometimes silence can be a way to punish or manipulate another, especially to get one's own way. For example, if a husband or wife wants to have a night out with his or her friends, a silent response might be a way the spouse is tacitly conveying disapproval or even trying to impart guilt. A negative silence, on the other hand, might indicate a lack of courage or convey a lack of support as, for example, when someone fails to join in condemning an injustice or when someone feels he or she is standing alone on an issue.

These are by no means the only negative uses of silences. Readers might reflect on their own experiences of hurtful or damaging silences and consider other examples from their own experience. We must always be on guard against these negative silences. This is surely not the kind of silence we are promoting and reflecting on in this book, nor the kind of silence we wish to learn better how to practice and make a habit in our everyday living. The silence we are considering here is a virtue.

The Positive Value and Doing of Silence

My very earliest memory of a sense of silence goes back to my preschool years. I was probably around age four—too old to take naps (unless I would spontaneously drift off), but too young to be in school. Each day after lunch, my older sister (when she wasn't in school), my younger brother, and I would be trundled off into the living room by our mother. We grew up in a household where the living room was sacrosanct—we children went in there to greet company, at Christmas, and other such special occasions. We never played in there. So, just to be ushered into the living room signaled to us this was special time in a special place. We were allowed to have coloring books and crayons or reading books—but definitely no toys. We knew this was not play time. We settled ourselves on the floor as Mom put some classical music on the old Victrola (ours was electric, not the crank kind!). She would lie on the couch for a nap and we children were left to our own devices for an hour: we could color or read our books, nap, daydream, play imaginary games in our head—but we could not talk or interact with each other (this is probably where we all learned to make faces at each other after Mom fell asleep!).

Little did I know that this practice—we probably did this for two or three years—would begin a lifetime habit of enjoying silence and appreciating it as a commodity in itself, far beyond mere absence of sound. Nor did I know that I also learned that silence came in many brightly colored packages, enticing our imaginations to vision new ways to re-create ourselves. As Max Picard intimates over and over again in *The World of Silence*, silence is not simply the absence of sound.[2] Josef Pieper makes the same point:

> Leisure is a form of silence, of that silence which is the prerequisite of the apprehension of reality; only the silent hear and those who do not remain silent do not hear. Silence, as it is used in this context, does not mean "dumbness" or "noiselessness"; it means more nearly that the soul's power to "answer" to the reality of the world is left undisturbed.[3]

Silence is a spiritual phenomenon as well as a physical phenomenon. We can stop talking or turn off the TV and still not be silent. We can stop our busy-ness and still not encounter the Sacred. Silence is that quality of life which earmarks greater attentiveness and awareness—God, self, others. By its very nature, silence brings us out of ourselves, for silence is a kind of *kenosis* (self-emptying) during which we rid ourselves of all which distracts us from single-mindedness about who we and others are and what we are about. In silence we "answer" the depths of meaning and being.

In the next four sections we explore more deeply both outward and inner silence. As always, we are interested in more than a theoretical exploration. We want to bring ourselves to a clear understanding of how a practice of silence in all its dimensions can be a good and necessary habit for self-fulfillment and deeper religious experience. There is no better motivation than this desire for personal and spiritual betterment.

1. Silence as Noise Stillness

Visitors to the Carlsbad Caverns in New Mexico are treated to a physical experience of silence as they are taken deep into the earth to experience the Caverns' unique beauty (this may happen while visiting other caves and caverns as well, I don't know; I experienced it at Carlsbad Caverns). At one point the guide has everyone stop still on the path, and warns those present that all the electric (unnatural) lights will be extinguished. We are told that the darkness will be so profound that even luminous watch dials are dark. After warning parents to grab onto the hands of their little ones tightly lest they be frightened, the lights are extinguished. What happens in the next few moments of absolute darkness is nothing short of amazing. Here a group of total strangers enter into a profound silence—so profound, in fact, that it is even a *tactile* experience: the silence can be touched, can be physically experienced. What is further amazing is that the normal movements and sounds of a group of human beings is also silent. Even the babies and small children are silent, unsounding witnesses of the physical impact the absence of visual stimulation can have on us.

As we said at the beginning of this chapter, silence is not merely the absence of sound. At the same time, eliminating or reducing the sounds around us is surely helpful. For one thing, with fewer sound waves hitting the ear drums, there is simply less stimulation. This diminishing of stimulation enables us to be more still. Audiologists have long been concerned about the decibel level of music concerts. I used to be abhorred at how portable cassette or CD players made it so easy to carry around sound all the time; that was before the age of the MP3 player, which now makes it even easier. We are a generation of noisy earbuds! And the young are not content just to *hear* the sounds—they do so at decibels so high that they can *feel* the sound as well. Both the sound and pulsing feeling are a pounding and almost constant stimulation for the whole body. Sound, however, isn't the only noise with which we surround ourselves.

Another ubiquitous presence of sound is now gathering around it a whole industry of etiquette beyond enormous profits for manufacturers and service providers. I'm referring here to the cell phone. The dangers of driving and talking on a cell phone (even with hands-free adaptors) have been well documented. And yet people still drive and use cell phones. Another aspect of the cell phone is more spiritual: we have developed a habit of thinking we must be one hundred percent available to family, work colleagues, friends. Now don't misunderstand: the cell phone has wonderful uses. Many parents gladly pay for their teenagers' cell phones because this is a way for them to be able to keep in touch with them. In emergencies cell phones can be a Godsend. But as with so many things in life, it is easy to turn a good thing into ubiquitous noise requiring new rules of etiquette. The "noise" of a cell phone evidences a compulsion always to be available. It also precipitates the embarrassment of having private conversations in places where others cannot help but overhear. Then there is the problem of just plain rudeness; to answer a cell phone when in the company of another is, basically, to say that the other is not all that important, certainly not so important as whoever is ringing— and that I'm so important others cannot do without me even for a few minutes. Cell phones require etiquette: when to turn them off and when to use them beneficially. When these two are not kept in balance, cell phones are just more noise in our lives.

In the last chapter we reflected on our frenetic lives. So, another way to look at "noise" is not so much in terms of sound as in terms of whatever is crowding in on us; taking over our lives; and commanding our attention, time, and energy.

Another source of this kind of "noise" is our perpetual busy-ness. Here I'm not speaking about purposeful activity. As human beings we work to make a living, prepare supper in order to nourish ourselves (for those who don't eat out every night), change the baby's diaper, clean our houses, exercise, and so on. Our lives are filled with needful and purposeful activities. Sometimes we might be able to streamline and eliminate some of the motions, but all of us have things we must do in order to live happy lives with relative ease and well-being. Another kind of busy-ness, however, is really more noise than anything else. That is the busy-ness with which we fill our lives in order to avoid the fine art of being comfortable with self or others. Leisure has become noisy group activity rather than quiet re-creating time and rest. No wonder we are exhausted all the time! Again, balance is in order. Sometimes a game of tennis is more important than sitting quietly (especially when it is an opportunity for friends to get exercise together or parents to spend time with children). At other times, frayed nerves and sharp tempers are signs warning us to slow down and calm down. The noise of activity must regularly give way to the hush of rest.

At a time when acquiring things is the norm, another noisy area in our lives is the sheer clutter of possessions. I know someone whose house is so full of knicknacks that my eyes never rest. They travel from one object to another unceasingly—there is no quiet space where my eyes can rest and I can be drawn into feeling at home. Consequently, I never rest when I am there. I know someone else whose house is a delight to visit. Artfully decorated, each object stands by itself with plenty of space around it. I can enjoy an art piece or decoration, and then my eyes can find rest to savor the enjoyment. The latter house is a delight to visit; the former is unsettling. Most of us have way more possessions than we ever could need. It's amazing how many families can have a garage sale every year and still never seem to run out of things to haul out of basement, garage, and attic. Some people are natural collectors—throwing away anything at all is like throwing away a piece of themselves. Maybe one response to all this clutter is simply to buy less. Shopping has actually become a noisy compulsion for some people. It is quieting to have the things we need, including not only the necessities of food, clothing, and shelter, but also of what salves our need for beauty: artful decorations; live green plants which constantly grow and change; objects of memory which keep present generations of loved ones, as well as mementos of the children's accomplishments in school (what parent's refrigerator doesn't have magnets holding prized grade school art!), or reminders of past trips or accomplishments. The difference between these objects and clutter is that art, plants, and mementos bring us into quiet; clutter takes us out of quiet into noise and restlessness.

We all have much noise in our lives. Some of it we cannot control, like the traffic on the streets or the baby crying. Much noise, however, we can control if we make a conscious choice to eliminate it. Assessing the unnecessary noise about us and extinguishing all we can is a first step in practicing the art of silence as noise stillness.

Reader Response Interlude

- My possessions which promote rest are . . . Those which leave me restless are . . .

- If I attack the unnecessary clutter in home and workplace, what will happen is . . .

- The time of day when I can enjoy sound-noise stillness is . . .

- I can prolong these moments if I . . .

- In order to form the habit of sound-noise stillness, with respect to the unnecessary noise in my life, I need to . . .

2. Silence as Body Stillness

Another aspect of outer silence is stilling our bodies. Without realizing it, most of us are perpetual motion machines. Even when we sleep, we tend to be restless. I know I've had a bad night when I have to remake almost completely my whole bed in the morning because while tossing and turning during the night I have pulled out all the sheets and covers.

I taught religion in Catholic high schools a number of years ago. At the beginning of a unit on prayer, I used to teach the youths (mostly sophomores) what I called the "silence exercise." I would take plenty of time, using plenty of examples, to talk about outer and inner silence with them. Then I would begin to practice silence with them. At first I only concentrated on outer silence, the easiest to grasp and control.

Noise stillness was relatively easy, except when sitting in absolute silence, we all became aware of how much sound truly still surrounded us: the buzz of the fluorescent lights, activity in the hall outside the classroom, and, invariably, the loud speaker would break in with an unexpected announcement. Usually this caused the class literally to jump in their seats, and we always got a good laugh out of it. Then we would start all over.

By far the most difficult outer silence for the youths to achieve was body stillness. This is especially difficult for boys of adolescent age; their bodies are growing and changing so fast (we adults could actually watch the pants climb up their legs month by month) and producing so much pent-up energy, that it could be actually physically painful for some of them to keep their bodies absolutely still. Any upper grade teacher knows how absent mindedly the students relentlessly click those ballpoint pens—and when too many of them are click-clicking all around the classroom, it can truly disturb the equilibrium (another noise to still).

If we take the time to notice, all of us have little habits we've fallen into which keep our bodies moving most of the time. We click our pens, swing our legs, cross and uncross our legs, play with our hair, scratch our heads, chew gum, rock in our chairs, drum our fingers on a table, tap out music playing in our heads, crack our knuckles—the list can go on and on. In themselves, none of these things are really wrong or bad. They do, however, affect our own bodies (much more than we would think) and can have a negative effect on those around us. For example, many of us have had the experience of sitting in a theater with the person in front of us constantly moving around in his or her seat and, consequently, we ourselves are constantly moving side to side so we can see around the individual.

One facet of body stillness is simply becoming aware of all our extraneous body movements and forming new habits of keeping our bodies still. These constant and unconscious body movements are difficult habits to break.

Another facet of body stillness involves relaxation. Without realizing it, many of us live with taut, strained muscles. There is good reason that massage therapy is so popular right now. Tight muscles are a form of body restlessness and are often a symptom of stress, which almost always seeks a physical release. Consciously relaxing our muscles is one way of being in body stillness.

Regular exercise is directly related to our ability to come to body stillness. Many of us exercise to keep in shape or lose weight; probably few of us have thought about the added body stillness benefits and how this is related to silence. Exercise releases pent-up energy and emotions, minimizes stress, increases the efficiency of our cardiovascular system, steps up our metabolism. All of this enables us to relax more in body stillness.

Outer silence (both noise stillness and body stillness) can become a habit only with concerted practice. Once it's habit, we find that outer silence is something we actually begin to crave, and we miss it when we don't have outer silence at least for a short period every day. Practicing outer silence before meeting with others can make the encounter much more fruitful because we are able to be much more attentive. Practicing outer silence before we fall asleep can promise us a much more restful night. Practicing outer silence before we eat can turn a simple meal into fine dining (and can even aid digestion). Practicing outer silence before working can make us wholesomely more productive.

To practice outer silence, all we need to do is turn off the radio or TV, find a place where we can be alone (although this exercise can be practiced with others as well, so long as everyone is agreeing to practice silence), sit where and how we can be comfortable, place our feet flat on the floor, fold our hands (to keep them from moving), become conscious of tight muscles and relax them, allow our breathing to slow down and become deliberately rhythmic, and then just sit . . . and sit . . . and sit. In the silence, we become aware of how relaxed we are, how good we feel, how energized we are. But most amazing is how this physical stillness leaves us joyful and content. In this outer silence, not only are we able to "answer" the world's reality, but we are able to be in touch with our own being, left undisturbed.

At the beginning, practicing noise and body stillness can be challenging. But like forming all habits, dogged perseverance is really the commitment which brings us to success. This noise and body stillness is the first aspect of silence to attain, but after forming this habit we are still only halfway. Now we turn to inner silence.

Reader Response Interlude

- My little habits of body motion are . . .

- I am aware of tight muscles when . . .

- When my body is still, I feel like . . .

- I do (or don't) exercise because . . .
  The benefits I feel (or miss) are . . .

- I resolve to set this time aside each day
  to practice outer noise and body
  stillness . . .

3. Silence as Mind Stillness

Outer silence is largely a matter of discipline. Inner silence (mind and soul still-ness) requires discipline, too, but that is not all there is to it. Inner silence is vari-ously gift, *kenosis*, self-giving, encounter, empty and full, sent and spent, life and death. Inner silence involves both seeking and receiving. Forming this habit, then, is much different from forming the habit of outer silence—and even far more challenging. At the same time, when inner silence becomes a habit for us, the delights it brings far exceed the demands it makes.

We humans have a singular capacity to think, and usually we have more than one thought at a time. Our minds are often racing, almost haphazardly flitting from recollection to task to feelings to desires to plans. We plan supper as we do the grocery shopping, listen to the youths tell us about their school day as we chop vegetables for salad, talk on the phone while we make out our grocery list, plan dates while we sit in class—we are becoming geniuses at multitasking and "multithinking."

Our mind freneticism does have its helpful or gratifying side. While doing routine tasks, we can put our minds to use planning other things, thinking through problems, looking at many sides of a decision with which we are faced. Or we can let our imaginations run wild—entertaining ourselves with stories. We can remember loved ones who have died or who are perhaps living far from us so we don't see them very often. Hence, "multithinking" isn't always undesirable. We do it quite naturally and comfortably. Nonetheless, it is possible that our minds run in so many directions at once that this mental frenzy diminishes the silence we are trying to make a habit in our lives. At times we need to slow our minds down. We need to come to mind stillness. We need to become single-minded.

Mind stillness isn't quite the same as focusing. We can be entirely focused, completely engrossed in some task, but still not experience mind stillness. This is especially true when the task we are doing is physically engaging us in such a way that our bodies are not still or at rest. For example, I might be focused on hanging a new picture—trying it in different places on the wall, deciding what works best for the aesthetics of the room, measuring so I get it up exactly right, making sure it is straight—but my mind and body are anything but still in the task because I am too anxious about what I am doing, getting it just right, not making a mistake that I may have to patch up later. On the other hand, we might be focused in such a way that our minds and bodies are very still. For example, we could be so engrossed in a beautiful sunset that for those few moments the whole world stops and the color and beauty become our entire reality. When this moment of mind and body stillness is over, we find ourselves refreshed and energized.

Mind stillness is a matter of releasing ourselves from all that presses in on us to relish in the luxury of, for this moment, all is right. Techniques are at hand to help us come to mind stillness. Those who practice mantra meditation, where a short group of words are said repeatedly, use it as a way to focus their minds and come to stillness. We carefully place art pieces or decorations in our homes as a way to focus and still our minds—for the moment of gazing, we are released of everything except what the art or decoration is presenting to us. Music can help focus others, especially when our attention is on the music and not on reading or doing some other task; in other words, when the music is enjoyed for its own sake rather than as background to something else we might be doing (like reading).

Mind stillness happens when we are not bombarded with an overload of sensory or mental stimulations. This raises an interesting question: can watching television bring us to mind stillness? Watching favorite TV programs might be relaxing, and can even help us let go of cares that burden us. Some TV programs are educational, some are clever, and some are just entertaining. The issue here is that TV watching involves multiple senses: auditory, visual, olfactory (if there is a scented candle nearby or time-release room fresheners), gustatory (snack foods are a favorite; TV dinners have become more sophisticated over the years, but many people eat meals in front of the TV), tactile (few people watch TV in straight chairs; we like our soft recliners). The spacing and length of commercials have made a science of keying into our sensory needs. Just because we are not aware of all that is bombarding us, doesn't mean that we are in any way still—in noise, body, or mind.

My experience has taught me that mind stillness can only be reached when we consciously set out to enter into this kind of stillness. It is rarely (if ever) a by-product of something else we might be doing. Mind stillness—in order for it to become a regular habit for us—must be consciously practiced regularly, surely daily. The best way to practice mind stillness is in conjunction with noise and body stillness. Enter into the outer stillness (suggestions were made above), and then consciously work at mind stillness. The easiest way is to have something meaningful on which we can focus (suggestions were also made above).

When practicing mind stillness with students in a classroom, I would remind them of the necessities of noise and body stillness, and get them into that outer, quiet mode. We would cough, stretch, place both feet on the floor, fold our hands, relax our muscles—do whatever we need to become outwardly still. Then we would use different approaches to help us focus, so that our minds could be still. A favorite was watching a candle (most states now have laws against burning candles in schools), but the students also enjoyed listening to soothing music (for some, this was their first experience of classical music) or gazing at an interesting art object. If they were having trouble sustaining single-mindedness, sometimes I would have them concentrate on the buzz of the fluorescent lights. At other times I would suggest a mantra (with adolescents, "I am loved" worked well), or even just a single word (I used *goodness, truthful, dignity*; sometimes, though, these words are loaded, and the students began thinking about different things rather than letting their minds become still). If someone is having trouble coming to mind stillness, sometimes it is good at the beginning of the exercise to let the mind wander for whatever time can be spared. This seems to be a good way to lay aside gently what is "on our minds" so that we can focus and become still.

Mind stillness is much more difficult to attain than noise or body stillness, partly because our minds are not so easily controlled as the sounds around us or our own bodies. We can't lay our minds on the table or put them in a soft recliner so they will be still. We can't turn off our minds like we can turn off the TV or MP3 player or put our feet on the floor and fold our hands. Perhaps, though, because mind stillness is so challenging, it is likewise so rewarding when we reach it. When our minds are still, our bodies naturally tend to become relaxed and still. In this kind of silence we settle comfortably into ourselves and come to peace and tranquility. In this kind of silence our truest and noblest selves are revealed; we see ourselves for who we are and come to believe we are very good.

By its very nature, mind stillness cannot be a habit we enter into all the time. Sometimes it is necessary to have many things on our mind; in fact, this "multi-thinking" probably characterizes most of our day. Mind stillness, then, is a habit we practice when we have the luxury of some free time to ourselves and is undertaken for its own sake. Interestingly enough, however, often emptying our mind to become single-minded is a great way to work out a knotty problem or overcome the consternation of stress. When we free our minds, often we ourselves are free.

Reader Response Interlude

- What is most often on my mind is . . .

- I am able to turn off distractions when . . .

- I experience mind stillness when . . .
    It makes me feel like . . .

- What enables me most to still my
    mind is . . .

- I need to still my mind when . . .

4. Silence as Soul Stillness

So far our consideration of silence—as noise, body, and mind stillness—has not regarded spiritual or religious dimensions. Another aspect of inner silence is soul stillness,[4] and we now turn specifically to the spiritual or religious. First, let's make a distinction between spiritual and religious.

"Spiritual," on the one hand, obviously refers to the spirit—that which is immaterial, generally beneficial, and brings us to wellness, wholeness, well-being. The spiritual is the non-sentient dimension of our personhood, the life-force which energizes us, the bigger-than-life part of us through which we rise above what is seen to participate in what is not seen. We might refer to spiritual values, spiritual energy, spiritual life, spiritual sisters and brothers, spiritual faith. All of these phrases (and there are others) bring out two important qualities of the spiritual: first, the spiritual encompasses a reality larger than ourselves; second, although the spiritual is intensely personal, it is usually not private. Spirituality is the way we live out our spirit—how we set priorities, what we believe and accept, how we transcend ourselves to be more than what appears. One can be spiritual without being religious, although in my experience most spiritual people are also religious.

"Religious," on the other hand, refers specifically to our relationship to a Divine Being, to God. The term *religious* derives from the Latin *religare* which means "to bind." To be religious means, therefore, to be bound to a higher being, as in a personal relationship. The religious person strives to encounter God and to experience God's presence and care, compassion and forgiveness. No matter how we name God, no matter what particular religious tradition we accept (three great religious traditions trace their roots to the biblical Abraham: Jews, Christians, and Muslims), we all share a common orientation to someone who creates and saves. We strive not only to have an intimate relationship with our God, but also to encounter the Divine as we journey toward our final, eternal inheritance.

Soul stillness is a value for both the spiritual and religious person. This is a silence in which we still our yearnings for mere self-satisfaction and fulfill our yearnings for self-transcendence. Soul stillness always takes us beyond ourselves into something larger than ourselves. Soul stillness also brings to our awareness our dearest beliefs—that to which we are committed and that which determines our worldview.

The three-consonant Hebrew root for *faith* is *'mn*, and in various grammatical forms it means "to be firm, constant, faithful, steadfast, honest," "to last, continue, trust"; all of these are relational terms implying endurance. This same Hebrew root gives us the word *amen*, meaning "certainly," "truly," "so be it." We end our prayers with amen—an acclamation declaring our belief, commitment, and adherence to what we have prayed. Another set of meanings for the three-consonant Hebrew root *'mn* is "to bring up, nurse, support." Here the word suggests a different kind of relationship—one of intimacy, familial bonds, sustenance. Soul stillness brings us to the reality of our life as gift and relationship. It brings us to the very heart of who we are where we can recognize our drive to be intimate with both Other and other.

Soul stillness prompts us to be in right relationship with others. It nourishes in us compassion and generosity, conviction and relevant action. Interestingly enough, soul stillness leaves us a bit restless in face of the great injustices some people perpetrate against other people (not just near around us, but all over the world), and the enormous ravaging of resources we permit. Soul stillness does not let us be isolated, but helps us be aware of the interconnectedness of all that is. Soul stillness is essential if we are to be persons of integrity.

Developing a habit of soul stillness is the most difficult silence to achieve. This fourth aspect of silence builds on the other three: noise, body, mind stillness. Essentially, the major difference between the practice of mind stillness and soul stillness is that in the latter we focus our attention specifically on the Divine. In practice, soothing music is replaced with sacred music. We might use a religious mantra to help us focus; for example, "God is good" or "Jesus saves" or "Allah is great." An aesthetic piece of art is replaced by sacred art. Another way to practice the habit of soul stillness is to do *lectio divina* (divine reading, especially of Holy Scriptures); *lectio divina* is such an important part of soul stillness that it is the focus of all of chapters 5 and 6.

Soul stillness is the most difficult aspect of silence because it is so illusive—the spirit is not at hand in the same way as noise, body, or even the mind. Soul stillness can leave us restless—above we remarked how it can spur us to right injustices and lead us to greater generosity toward those less fortunate than ourselves. Soul stillness can also leave us restless because in its silence we face ourselves, with all pretensions drifting off into the hush. Here we face our strengths and weaknesses, our grace and sinfulness. Here we encounter the utter love and compassion of God and realize that all we are and do is pure gift of the Divine. Ultimately, soul stillness reduces us to true humility (the root of which is *humus*, earthy)—where we return to be embraced and re-created by God into ever more perfect images of the goodness of creation and of the Divine.

Reader Response Interlude

- I most yearn for spiritual fulfillment when . . .

- I name God . . .

- Soul stillness is easiest for me when . . . most difficult when . . .

- In soul stillness, I learn . . . about myself; I learn . . . about God.

- To strengthen a habit of soul stillness, I need to . . .

Making Silence a Habit

When I would begin explaining and practicing silence with my students, the group could last only about forty-five seconds the first few times we tried it.[5] With practice, as silence became more a habit, on average each class could comfortably reach about twenty minutes in absolute stillness. I knew I had achieved something positive when they would come to class—long after we had moved onto another unit of study—and ask if they could do the "silence exercise." Years later I might by chance meet some of them who would tell me that they still practiced their silence exercise. I would leap for joy within myself—clearly this had become a habit for them.

Habits take hold of us when we do something over and over again. The more difficult the task, the longer it will take for the habit to be well established. Since silence is so utterly countercultural, it is not surprising that the habit of silence does not come easily nor quickly. It is something we must consciously introduce into our lives, and then keep at it even if we are interrupted, distracted, overwhelmed with duties and responsibilities. When time challenged, the "luxuries" of our lives are the first things to go; and so it stands to reason that when time challenged, our time for silence can so easily fall by the wayside. This is, in fact, the most important time not to give up, but to remain faithful to our forming habit of silence.

In this chapter we laid out four aspects or dimensions of silence, and discussed them linearly—one after another. In actual practice, they tend to roll up into one experience. Or sometimes only one dimension (noiselessness, for example) is needed at a particular moment, and that is sufficient. What has become clear to me over the years is that for fruitful prayer and life-giving encounter with God to happen, all four dimensions of silence must become part of the very prayer. Without outer and inner stillness, our prayer is largely one distraction after another. With outer and inner stillness, our prayer is the embodiment of the psalmist's invitation, "Be still, and know that I am God!" (Psalm 46:10). And to that, we say amen!

NOTES

1. Abraham J. Heschel, *Man's Quest for God: Studies in Prayer and Symbolism* (New York: Charles Scribner's Sons, 1954) 44.

2. See, for example, Max Picard, *The World of Silence*, pref. Gabriel Marcel, trans. Stanley Godwin (Wichita, Kansas: Eighty Day Press, 2002 [originally published in English by Regnery Gateway, 1952]) 15, 17, 22–23, 198–99.

3. Josef Pieper, *Leisure: The Basis of Culture*, intro. T. S. Eliot, trans. Alexander Dru (New York and Toronto: The New American Library, Inc., A Mentor Book, 1963 [1952]) 41.

4. I use *soul* here not necessarily in the Aristotelian sense of the body-soul dichotomy, but as a way to designate that which can be spirit and/or religious. I avoided *spirit stillness* so that those readers who do not consider themselves "religious" can still find themselves in these reflections.

5. The thumb-nail rule I would use is when I saw three people move, then I would call the exercise to an end. Usually it would take a few seconds for the group to enter deeply into silence; it is always "audible" when this deep silence is achieved.

PART TWO
Silence and Everyday Praying

CHAPTER 4

From Earthy Silence to Sacred Encounter

So I sing your glory;
I am not silent.
O LORD my God,
I will give thanks to you forever.[1]

Every other fall semester I teach an introductory course in liturgy and prayer. One class in particular kept expressing its hunger for a sense of the mystery of God during liturgy and prayer. Much to my surprise, during one class the participants quite spontaneously began to ask questions which led them to share quite openly about their personal relationship with God. As they learned more and more about liturgy and its riches, they related that they felt I had "ruined" them. What once had been a healthy and satisfying prayer life was now pretty much in shambles. They said God felt absent from them. Even in relating this, they knew what my response would be: this might be called the "dark night of the soul," and some of the mystics experienced it for very long periods. They groaned in one voice. When they asked me how they should now pray, I suggested they might perhaps thank God for this seeming absence, because it is surely a harbinger of a newer and deeper relationship, one that gets them even closer to the mystery they desire to embrace.

Again, a collective groan was uttered, but they grasped quite clearly what I was trying to convey. Spiritual growth is often preceded by emptiness, and a sentiment of gratitude is not for the emptiness but for God's working strangely and marvelously within us. For most of us, encountering God does not come easily, and so neither does prayer. A less difficult task which helps our growing in prayer is developing a habit of silence. Into this silence the light of Divine Presence gradually breaks forth, and deeper sacred encounter in prayer becomes possible—the kind of soundless conversation which is endlessly satisfying and prodigiously fruitful.

In spite of so much hype over our materialistic, secular, a-theistic society, it is still taken for granted that most people are religious—they acknowledge a higher being and seek to have at least some minimal relationship with that being. Many people may be disenchanted with various organized religions, but that is not the same as being a-religious or non-religious. Polls, moreover, show that a good number of people in the United States of America still regularly go to church for communal worship, with about one-third going almost weekly. We have a constitutional separation of church and state, yet it seems that most people manage to balance the two and appreciate both church and state in their everyday living. Even if we do not regularly attend formal worship services, our hearts naturally turn to God, especially at times of great joy or deep sorrow. As we experience so many good things around us, we cannot be silent; our hearts well up in praise and thanksgiving.

The media was quick to report that immediately after September 11, 2001, church attendance in the U.S.A. skyrocketed. The media coverage often zeroed in on those rabbis, priests, and ministers who were attentive to the spiritual needs of the dead, dying, seriously injured, the weary rescue personnel. The World Trade Center's first official victim is #0001—the number recorded on Father Mychal (Michael) F. Judge's death certificate. Literally overnight, Father Mike became a household name across the country. That simple, generous Franciscan priest who was chaplain to the New York City Fire Department immediately went to the World Trade Center to minister spiritual care when he heard of the disaster. He lost his own life while serving others, thus becoming a victim himself. Catholics, Protestants, Jews, Muslims, atheists, a-theists alike admired the self-sacrificing compassion of this priest. During these kinds of soul-wrenching events we need someone to assure us of God's continued care and love.

As easy as it seems to be to turn to God in times of great joy and/or sorrow, it seems equally as difficult to sustain a satisfying relationship with God during the ordinariness of daily living. Joseph Pieper comments that

> the meaning of celebration . . . is man's affirmation of the universe and his experiencing the world in an aspect other than its everyday one. Now we cannot conceive a more intense affirmation of the world than "praise of God," praise of the Creator of this very world.[2]

Even when our experience of the world is a sad or difficult one, we still tend to turn to God and affirm our connection to the world through even lamentable events. The critical question becomes: Can we affirm our world (and lives) in simple, everyday events? The challenge for answering this question affirmatively is that we must begin to see God in the ordinary and lift up the ordinary to a participation in divine glory.

If the world is sacred because of the holiness of the Creator, then in a sense there is nothing which is "ordinary." Every thing and every event can move us to recognize Divine Presence. Even when God seems far away, we know the Divine is near, for everyone and everything around us is ultimately a gift of divine love and care.

Silence is a privileged way to raise our awareness of the sacredness of the ordinary. In silence we are able to gain perspective in such a way that we can practice the "silence of *waiting*,"[3] to use Rudolf Otto's words. Otto goes on to explain what he means by this waiting: "It means our submergence, i.e. inward concentration and detachment from the manifold outward distractions . . . ."[4] Before the silence of waiting leads us to Sacred Presence, it empties us and prepares us. The silence of waiting is a kind of dark night of the soul, during which we anticipate the spiritual growth which brings us to a deeper relationship with our God.

Imbued with a new perspective of silence and waiting, we begin to see that the earthiness and ordinariness of our everyday living is but another side to an abiding Sacred Presence. The ordinary and sacred collapse into a life of spirit and mystery in which we come face to face with the holiness of God. The only thing that should break our profound silence in face of the awesome holiness of the Divine Majesty is the heart-felt praise and thanksgiving we humbly utter to God. *This* is what breaks our silence: utter amazement at the sheer goodness and fidelity of God toward us. *This* is what breaks our silence: the astounding realization that the God of all creation is attentive to each of us creatures. *This* is what breaks our silence: the startling revelation that all earthy silence is really sacred silence.

Learning to Crave Sacred Silence

Sacred silence is hardly something that comes easily or automatically at either prayer or worship or—with even more difficulty—in daily living. We must teach ourselves the habit of valuing sacred silence, and discover the riches it offers. Like the value of silence in general on which we've been reflecting, sacred silence requires of us commitment and discipline if it is to become a habit. Further, because much of our sacred silence is part of worship—a communal experience— there is the added challenge of our dependence upon others who are present with their own valuing (or non-valuing) of sacred silence. We are less in control with sacred silence, but the outcome is even far richer, for it brings us to the depths of mystery.

The best way to achieve and value sacred silence during worship is to practice earthy silence as a habit of our daily living. Many parents teach their children discipline and good behavior through "time out" periods—when they are squirrely or defiant or doing something they shouldn't, the children are given a time out period away from others during which they can think about their behavior and decide to make other choices.

One afternoon while caring for my two grand nieces, I learned the value of this time out silence from the older one. She was to take a nap after lunch, but when we finished eating she insisted that we finish watching the movie we had begun before lunch. I was firm in my "No, it's nap time," and she came very close to throwing a temper tantrum. I turned from her and began to take care of the baby, when all of a sudden she disappeared and things became awfully quiet. I found her in the kitchen, standing in a corner. When I asked her what she was doing, she said, "Aunt Joyce, I just need time out to get rid of my bad mood and do what you are asking me." Sure enough, even before I was finished with the baby, she came in, tears wiped away, and announced that she was ready to take a nap so we could finish the movie when she got up.

A similar time out period is necessary for older children, youths, and young and older adults. When we feel tense and testy, we need to take "time out"—just a few minutes to gather ourselves, to become quiet inside, to calm down and re-focus, to make decisions. If these "time out periods" spent in earthy, ordinary silence become a natural habit of our daily living, then when silence is introduced at specific times during worship, we are perfectly comfortable with it and know how to use this precious time to focus ourselves on God in a different way from how we are present to God during the rest of the service or during our daily living.

Sacred silence tends to be limited or overlooked altogether during too many of our worship services. We think that worship means we must be proactive in offering our praise and thanksgiving to God. Yet, during moments of sacred silence we can speak to God our very personal prayers during which we have an opportunity to unburden our weary hearts and free our troubled minds. Also during the silence we can be attentive to God in a different way, hearing divine words which encourage and strengthen us. Sometimes during the silence we are simply still, basking in Divine Presence and receiving nurture from it. Because such important personal prayer takes place during the sacred silence of worship, we ought to desire that sacred silence become more and more a regular part of the worship service. In the sacred silence we gradually become aware of how indispensable silence is in order for worship truly to accomplish its purpose—to facilitate an encounter in praise and thanksgiving with our good God who saves us and blesses us with unimaginable new life.

One key to learning to crave sacred silence is *memory*. Memory is not simply "recalling" a past event, but an active retrieval of the import of a past event, a kind of retrieval which makes the past event present in all its meaning and power. Thus, when Jewish people celebrate Passover, they are not simply recalling an event that happened several millennia ago; they are making present in their lives and celebrating in the here and now God's mighty saving deeds of bringing them from slavery to freedom—both personally and as a nation. When Christians celebrate the Lord's Supper, they are not simply recalling what Jesus did with his disciples on that night before he died; they are making present in their lives and celebrating in the here and now Jesus' profound gift of himself to his disciples. Memory teaches us to crave silence because in the recollection spawned by silence we are able to appreciate so much more fully the event(s) or person(s) we remember. Without the silence, the meaning and power of past events stay in the past. With silence, they become active forces in shaping us into that which we profess as religious persons.

Reader Response Interlude

- I feel myself craving silence when . . .
  I crave sacred silence when . . .

- I unburden myself best to God as I . . .

- Silence shapes me as a religious person
  in that . . .

- My best memories are . . . My most
  significant sacred memories are . . .
  They happen most often when . . .

Why Silence during Prayer?

Prayer can mean many things to different people, and *how* we pray can be even more diverse. At the very least, prayer is a personal presence—encounter—between the praying person and God. Russian Orthodox monk Anthony Bloom puts it this way: "First of all, it is very important to remember that prayer is an encounter and a relationship, a relationship which is deep, and this relationship cannot be forced either on us or on God."[5] Another way to describe prayer is that it is *basking in Divine Presence.* This last statement implies that the heart of prayer is God's coming to us and our awakening to that advent. The real "work" of prayer is our becoming open to Divine Presence.

We have all been party to "one-way" conversations: the one dominates a conversation so that others cannot get a word in. These conversations quickly become quite boring to us. One possible reason why it is so difficult for so many well-intentioned, good people to remain faithful to daily prayer is that it becomes tedious—yes, even boring. We tend to turn our prayer into "one-way" conversations with God, and when we run out of things to say (usually asking for our needs) we don't know what to do. Introducing periods of silence into our personal prayer (at the same time that we note that there is certainly nothing wrong in itself with our *speaking* during prayer) is a way to let go of prayer as a "one-way" conversation and consciously choose to make prayer an attentiveness to Presence. These moments of silence during prayer have at least four practical purposes.

First, silence during prayer brings us face to face with our longing for God, especially when from time to time God seems to be absent no matter how hard we try to be open to God's presence (who is, after all, always present to us). Anthony Bloom reminds us that

> the day when God is absent, when he is silent—that is the beginning of prayer. Not when we have a lot to say, but when we say to God, "I can't live without you, why are you so cruel, so silent?" This knowledge that we must find or die—that makes us break through to the place where we are in the Presence. If we listen to what our hearts know of love and longing and are never afraid of despair, we find that victory is always there on the other side of it.[6]

This perceived absence of God (as mentioned above, this is what the classical mystics referred to as the "dark night of the soul") and patiently sitting in the silent void can be a prayer in itself. Whenever our prayer is not satisfying (that is, when we don't have a concrete sense of God's presence to us), it is always tempting to think we are not very good at praying, to skip prayer, or give up altogether because we don't think the prayer is leading anyplace, much less to God. Instead, the silent void can teach us a different kind of prayer: patient waiting which empties us and opens us. In the silent void we learn much about ourselves and our relationship to God. Thus, we are learning much about prayer itself. We are learning how the absence and waiting beckon us to let go of our present forms of prayer and prepare us for something new, something which brings an entirely new or certainly deeper relationship with the Divine One.

Second, silence during prayer aids *recollection*, which helps to draw us into prayer in such a way that we let go of our everyday distractions and surrender ourselves to Divine Presence and encounter. Recollection draws us to discard whatever keeps us from "re-collecting" ourselves for the single purpose for which we pray: to give God praise and thanks, to lift our hearts to God, to present our needs, to be attentive to God's abiding presence to us. Recollection enables us simply to settle down, to stop the sounds, and to remember why we have chosen to take this time to pray. Prayer silence as recollection helps us to be present to God because it places God at the very center of who we are and what we are doing at that moment.

Third, silence during prayer aids *meditation*, which fosters our absorption of God's word and saving deeds on our behalf. Surely, to hear God well and even begin to comprehend the depths of what God speaks to us urges us to pause and ponder. God's word is dynamic and mysterious, prophetic and messianic, emptying and fulfilling. A few brief moments of sacred silence are hardly enough to catch the richness of what God speaks to us; this is one reason why using Sacred Scriptures during prayer is so helpful. Meditation enables us to still our minds, bodies, and souls in such a way that we become attentive to God's overtures of divine speech, spoken to us personally in the depths of our hearts. In this divine quiet does God speak to us about the exciting, new, and saving life. In the divine quiet do we catch God's speaking to us. But this can happen only if we quiet ourselves in intense silence so that we can hear.

Fourth, silence during prayer brings forth the most authentic, full-throated *praise*. Any encounter with the Divine kindles in us an overwhelming and overflowing desire to shout out from our filled hearts. From the silence of the intersection of life experience and Divine encounter flows an irresistible need to speak—nay, shout—out our response to such love and intimacy, care and compassion, mercy and forgiveness. Isn't it telling that even praise is a gift God gives to us? Even in the praise as we speak, sing, or shout to God, the Divine is quietly whispering to each of us in the depths of our hearts.

Why silence during prayer? The answer is really quite simple: without the silence we risk missing the Divine Presence, missing the gifts God offers to us in our prayer.

Reader Response Interlude

- I experience a silent void in my prayer most often when . . .

- My prayer is most fulfilling when . . .

- I seem to be predisposed to encounter God in prayer when . . .

- My richest prayer has been . . . because . . .

- For my prayer to grow, I need to . . .

Why Silence during Worship?

Prayer in itself is truly worship—a conscious giving to God of our reverence and adoration. When we hear the word *worship,* however, we usually think of the more formal, communal gatherings in a church, house church, meeting house, synagogue, or temple. This worship often follows some sort of structure or repeated patterns of essential elements. Generally speaking, worship rightly and always unfolds (not necessarily in this order) with the sounds of greeting each other, song and instruments, praise prayer and intercessory prayer, communal body movement and thanksgiving prayer, dismissal and blessing prayer. Less often does worship include longer, intense moments of utter silence during which we experience the advent of the Almighty.

Not all silences during worship have the same purpose. The most important silences during worship are what we might call "reflective silences." These are distinct periods of quiet during the service when we are given the luxury of time to savor in our hearts the communal prayer and make particular its sentiments, allowing our own personal needs and desires to be uniquely expressed to God. A silence following the proclamation of God's word enables us to hear these truly as sacred words and allow the scriptures to become for us scintillating divine speech—God's dynamic words spoken to us in the context of *now* which enlighten us and bring comfort and peace, challenge and command. A silence following the sermon or homily can help us appropriate the words of the preacher or homilist so that they become our own words and a mandate to live the next week differently because of what we have heard. A silence after a hymn or anthem can help the singing be more than *voicing* our praise, but also give us time to pay as much attention to the text as to the melody. Silence after Communion opens for us the space deep within our hearts sentiments of adoration and thanksgiving.

Exactly where these reflective silences (and how many of them) are inserted into the worship service is either determined by the religious tradition or by the structure of the service itself. Too many silences or too prolonged a silence can disrupt the natural rhythmic flow of the service. No silence or not enough silence can turn the worship service in on the congregation members, making worship more self-fulfilling than self-emptying praise and thanksgiving.

Secondarily (but not unimportant), another kind of silence during worship is what we might call "transitional silence." This silence enables us to adjust ourselves to a different mind set when the focus or action during worship shifts. There may be a shift between gathering and an opening prayer, between proclamation of the word and sermon or homily, between prayer and announcements, between intercession and blessing. A brief, transitional silence helps the congregation "shift gears" and become ready for the next movement of the service. These transitional silences help bring out the differing styles and purposes of various elements that make up the worship service. Silence during worship has nothing at all to do with slowing down or hurrying up the prayer. Silent periods are always inserted at key moments to enable us to pray and worship better.

Few worship traditions celebrate without music or with minimal music. We might think of music—since it is the sound of both instruments and the human voice—as opposed to silence, but music itself has its own kind of silence. Max Picard goes so far as to claim that even music itself is silence:

> The sound of music is not, like the sound of words, opposed, but rather parallel to silence.
> It is as though the sounds of music were being driven over the surface of silence.
> Music is silence, which in dreaming begins to sound.
> Silence is never more audible than when the last sound of music has died away.[7]

It is true that there are rests written into musical compositions, but when we speak of music as silence, we are not referring to these rests. Rather, we are referring to music's power to do what silence itself does: it "allows the assembled community of disciples to come to the point of *niente*, that pregnant nothingness that is a presence to everything."[8] The sound of music is the very contrast of silence and serves to deepen the silence in our worship. Without music the silence cannot be heard. It is no mistake that all the great religious traditions use that particular kind of music which we call "chant." In chant the repeated and limited number of notes and the emphasis on breathing lull us into the sacred silence essential for Divine encounter. When we begin to think of the music in our worship as anticipating silence and giving birth to silence, then we have come to understand the great mystery of worship's necessity for silence.

Reader Response Interlude

- Worship for me is . . .

- I feel the need for sacred silence during worship when . . .

- I miss silence during worship when . . .

- Sacred silence during worship is most fruitful for me when . . .

- When I have opportunities for silence during worship, I . . .

Silence's Sacred Speech

What dignity we have: the Divine One speaks to us. Sometimes our deity speaks to us in a still, small, whispering, even silent voice (see 1 Kings 19:11–13); sometimes God speaks in a loud, booming, unmistakable, commanding voice (see Deuteronomy 5:22–27). Whether silent, nearly silent, or unmistakably loud and clear, God does speak to those who listen, and the sacred speech is always energizing, life-giving, life-changing, self-revealing. The issue, therefore, isn't whether God speaks; the issue is whether we dispose ourselves to listen and whether we appropriate the sacred speech and live God's desire for us. Silence is one way to dispose ourselves to hear sacred speech.

Sacred speech is revealing in silence because the quiet affords the most contrast for the different modality of sacred speech. God does not talk to us as we are used to articulation (and if we hear voices, we probably ought to start worrying about ourselves). Sacred speech is a prompting, an urge, an inclination which moves us to deeper belief, greater compassion, gracious charity, speedier forgiveness, and more just actions. It may come in the form of proclaimed scriptures, witness of others, personal inclination. The many "voices" coalesce in a single and familiar comfort: we know we are loved and offered divine mercy.

For us Christians, God has spoken most profoundly to us in the Word made flesh. In Jesus Christ the Divine is present among us and within us. Through the Incarnation the Divine dwells among us in a wholly new and unprecedented way. In becoming like us in all things, save sin, Jesus Christ, by assuming humanity, raises us up to share in divinity. In the silence and darkness of night was Jesus born unto us in rank poverty devoid of the clutter of noise (except the soft chatter of the stable animals) or possessions (the newborn baby was laid in a manger) (see Luke 2:6–8). In the silence and light of a new dawn are we ourselves reborn to share in his saving mystery. Only in this silence do we—*can* we—hear the word spoken to us and encounter the Word present to us in enlightening and life-giving sacred speech.

The deity speaks to us in sacred speech. But there is the other side: as we conform ourselves more perfectly to God's will (and as we Christians conform ourselves more to the Body of Christ into which we are baptized), we ourselves become and *are* sacred speech for others. Not only (and perhaps least) our words, but also our *actions* speak of God's presence or absence. Our relationship with God is not only a personal one, but is one that affects those in our faith community as well as all those we touch by the goodness of our lives. This kind of witness does not have as its purpose proselytizing, but rather simply pouring forth for all to see the goodness with which God has blessed us. Thus do we become a blessing for others.

Silence not only creates the milieu for us to encounter God, but it teaches us how to utter sacred speech for the good of others. In this we can all be prophets—those covenant servants called by God to be icons of fidelity in the community. We can be the light that dispels darkness and brings hope and consolation to others. We can be peacemakers because we have encountered, heard, and spoken the stillness of divine speech. Our lives need silence. God always accommodates us. All we need do is open ourselves to the divine voice calling us into Divine Presence, speaking to us in the depths of our hearts, encouraging us to be speakers of the divine word.

NOTES

1. Psalm 30; translation from Joyce Ann Zimmerman, CPPS, et al., *Pray without Ceasing: Prayer for Morning and Evening* (Collegeville: Liturgical Press, 1993) 173.

2. Josef Pieper, *Leisure: The Basis of Culture*, intro. T. S. Eliot, trans. Alexander Dru (New York and Toronto: The New American Library, Inc., A Mentor Book, 1963 [1952]) 56.

3. Rudolf Otto, *The Idea of the Holy: An Inquiry into the Non-rational Factor in the Idea of the Divine and its Relation to the Rational*, trans. John W. Harvey (London, Oxford, New York: Oxford University Press, 1971 [1923]) 211; italics in original.

4. Otto, *The Idea of the Holy*, 211.

5. Archbishop Anthony Bloom, *Beginning to Pray*, (New York, Paramus, Toronto: Paulist Press, 1970) 2.

6. Bloom, *Beginning to Pray*, Introduction, xvii.

7. Max Picard, *The World of Silence*, pref. Gabriel Marcel, trans. Stanley Godwin (Wichita, Kansas: Eighty Day Press, 2002 [originally published in English by Regnery Gateway, 1952]) 27.

8. Kathleen Harmon, "The General Intercessions As Liturgical '*Niente*,'" *Liturgical Ministry* 2 (Winter 1993), 28; *niente* is a dynamic term in music, roughly translated as "nothing" or "no sound," different from the musical rest in that the musician is engaged in making sound but so softly that the sound cannot be heard. See also her essay, "The Silence of Music," *Liturgical Ministry* 10 (Spring 2001) 93–100.

CHAPTER 5

Praying Silence with LECTIO DIVINA

For speaking and teaching belong to the master; the disciple's part is to be silent and to listen.[1]

So many centuries ago the father of Western monasticism, Saint Benedict, understood well the necessity of silence in order to curb the tongue's rogue tendencies, to predispose us to listen with our hearts as well as our ears, to foster our contemplation of what matters most deeply to us. Even today, as Benedictine Abbot Gregory Polan observes, "people flock to monasteries for days of recollection, weekend retreats, and time to break the incessant noises that invade their lives."[2] At the same time, Max Picard laments that

> it is true that silence still exists as a true silence in monastic communities. In the Middle Ages the silence of the monks was still connected with the silence of other men outside the monastery. Today the silence in the monasteries is isolated; it lives literally only in monastic seclusion.[3]

We notice in these two citations a tension between our desire and need for silence (Polan) and the unappeasable call to frenzied sound and activity (Picard). One way to satisfy our desire and need for quiet and break the cycle of hustle and bustle is to allow monastic silence to re-connect with us. Monastics—Catholic, Protestant, Buddhist—can all serve as icons of silence for us and teach us how to hear God in the habit of our silence. They can remind us that without quiet and rest our daily activities rule us rather than serve us and others and our common good. Monastics can help us to do with silence as they do: use it for recollection, that "re-collecting" of ourselves into centered beings who know the meaning of life and our ultimate goal—eternal life.

Obviously, I am not recommending that everyone become a monastic. However, forming the habit of silence is valuable for everyone, and becoming immersed in God's word so that we can better hear God speak is an essential practice if we wish to grow in the spiritual life. In the Middle Ages the monasteries were center points for the people; they attended religious services in the large monastic churches, to be sure, but the monastery compound was also a beehive of trades, learning, and the arts. The people regularly rubbed shoulders with the monks, learned from them, and imbibed their silent and God-filled spirit. Even today in their relative seclusion, monastics can teach us much about silence and the necessity of hearing well God's word in order to lead good and purposeful lives.

This chapter shifts from the reflective focus of the previous chapters; now we are about praying silence, but we do so using a particular prayer method. *Lectio divina*, as a distinctive kind of praying, is definitive of some monasteries, especially Benedictine ones, and is a special pathway to conversion. *Lectio divina* is an invitation to "continual conversion of life" because there is "a dynamism in the word of God that renew[s] and re-create[s] people, with God's word forming them by its own unique and mysterious power." Further, as Abbot Polan hastens to say, "And yet, is that [conversion] not what we, whether a monk or any Christian, hope to find in our reading of the Scriptures. . . . If so, the practice of *lectio divina* has something wonderful to offer anyone who practices it."[4] Opportunities for some actual experiences of *lectio divina* comprise the content of the next chapter. Using 15 selections from sripture, the reader is invited into silence and to do *lectio divina* (divine reading).

Further, each of the scripture passages of the 15 opportunities for *lectio divina* were deliberately chosen to illustrate an important facet of silence. Thus these invitations to *lectio divina* are more than opportunities for prayer or even guidance for delving more deeply into God's word encountered in silence. They help us understand better how silence, in all its mystery and fullness, can be revealed in so many ways. These scripture passages teach us more about the value of silence and how silence is virtue-birthing. In this way even our praying is an opportunity to learn more about silence and deepen our habit of silence. Our *lectio divina*, then, helps us form the habit of silence and treasure more deeply and effectively God's word, as well as nurtures us in our appreciation of silence itself and the wonderful fruits that come from it.

Spiritual writers throughout the centuries have put forward different steps or methods for practicing *lectio divina*. Two prerequisites are common to the tradition: first, one must become silent (both outer and inner) before one begins with scripture reading; and second, *lectio* is not just reading a sacred text, but is an intense and prayerful engagement with the text. Quantity here isn't the issue; the scriptures are a vehicle for Divine encounter. With these prerequisites in mind, Abbot Polan outlines four progressive steps in the practice of *lectio divina*:

1) *lectio* (reading, usually out loud);
2) meditation (reflecting or meditating on the text or a part of it);
3) prayer (praying *from* the text); and
4) contemplation (deep communion with God).[5]

The second step, meditation, needs a bit more explanation. It may help the *lectio* process and open the space for greater insight if the person has some knowledge about the sacred text, but this is not absolutely necessary. Nor is *lectio* an exegetical exercise, that is, a formal exercise in explaining and interpreting a sacred text. The meditation process is more about the individual gaining personal insight into God's word which leads to prayer: what is the text saying *to me at this time*? What is God saying to me at this time? *Lectio* affords a more relaxed approach to text interpretation. Misinterpretation of sacred texts is always a concern, but this should not quell our imaginations during *lectio*.

Whether undertaken alone or with others, *lectio divina* always leaves us vulnerable. When alone, we are vulnerable before God: with our weaknesses and failings, our strengths and goodness; we are called to honesty and integrity—if we cannot fool God about our real selves, this is the time not to try to fool ourselves, either. When practicing *lectio* with others, we are especially vulnerable and must trust that others will respect what we share and not judge us. Vulnerability in turn brings us to greater trust and honesty, both with ourselves and with others.

In the 15 scripture selections that follow in the next chapter, I am inviting the reader into my own personal practice of *lectio* (as much as is possible through a printed medium). For each one, the scripture is printed out for the convenience of the reader (*reading*); one might read a passage more than once, and reading out loud is very helpful so one can listen to the words. If a particular word or phrase pops out and begs to be savored, then do that; the quantity of words one reads is not important. I include a brief *meditation* with each passage, which helps us open ourselves to prayer and an encounter with God as well as points to a particular facet or outcome of silence. Hopefully, the reader is also drawn to supply his or her own meditation words and images; don't be hampered by the text. These meditations are given as a guide, not as a final product. The meditations given here are simply to get the process started. Finally, I conclude each practice in *lectio divina* with a *prayer*; again, the reader is also encouraged to use his or her own words for this prayer. Obviously, the fourth and final step in the *lectio* process—contemplation or communion with God—is impossible to convey through print media. I leave it to the reader to be open to that fourth step and experience God's presence, however it may come.

A slightly different method might be helpful if a group (for example, a small faith-sharing group) wishes to practice *lectio divina* together. The four steps outlined above would still be in place, but with some slight variation. Here is a suggested, slightly amended method for group use:

1) someone in the group slowly, out loud, reads the chosen passage;

2) pause for quiet reflection or meditation;

3) during a second out loud reading of the sacred text, the group is asked to become intensely aware of any word or phrase that strikes them;

4) anyone in the group who wishes might share her or his word or phrase, but no one adds commentary or comments, and the people in the group would not share in any particular order (that is, don't go around a circle, forcing someone to share; if someone wishes not to share, that is fine);

5) the group once again observes some silence, allowing the Holy Spirit to work in individuals and the group as a whole;

6) anyone who wishes is invited to pray aloud; all are invited to pray quietly in their hearts;

7) finally, another more lengthy silence is observed in which members might move into contemplation. There could be a common final prayer.

Reader Response Interlude

- Prayer means to me . . .

- I pray best when . . .

- I am most inclined to try a new prayer form when . . .

- I think *lectio divina* may help me in that . . . It is appealing to me in that . . .

Moving toward Doing *Lectio Divina*

There are many passages besides these in the Sacred Scriptures that can draw us into God's presence and lift our souls in worship. *Lectio divina* is a way to savor God's word in our hearts, let it seep deep within our souls, and guide and motivate us toward goodness all our lives. *Lectio divina* is a way of silent praying, of uniting ourselves to God's spoken word in an unsounded way.

Our meditations on God's word and Word in the next chapter open us to many different characteristics of silence. As we do *lectio divina* we become more aware of the many ways silence helps us, and the many ways silence touches us and teaches us. Silence is so much more than an absence of sound. When embraced for all its positive qualities, silence is the balm that soothes our being, encourages our spiritual growth, and sustains sacred encounter.

Lectio divina itself is a way into silence and a kind of spirituality, one with God's word at its center. This spirituality of the word is not so much concerned with words as it is with pouring our hearts out to a God who listens patiently to all we say—and especially to all we don't say. When using God's word for prayer, God's words become our own words; God's voice becomes our voice; God's ways more perfectly become our ways. Words can be nothing . . . a tinkling cymbal, a clanging bell, a pounding drum. But when those words are divine words—inspired by our scriptures or God's words spoken directly within our hearts—then they are a full orchestra executing *niente* perfectly. Out of ourselves, ever so slowly, God draws the words that comfort, heal, forgive, strengthen, bless us. Worshipping silence is our response.

The 15 examples of *lectio divina* given in chapter 6 have no introductory words or explanations; enough has been said about *lectio divina* in this chapter for the reader to begin without further ado. Let each doing of *lectio* stand on its own. It may be helpful if the reader takes one at a time, perhaps covering them over a couple of weeks; simply reading them one after another as we read the other pages of this book would not give the reader an actual experience of *lectio divina*. Don't hurry through chapter 6; this is not for reading or learning as such. It is for praying. I also recommend that the last chapter be saved until after all 15 practices of *lectio divina* have been tried, practiced, and prayed.

One final introductory remark: *Lectio divina* need not end with the completion of these 15 prayer opportunities. The reader may want to choose his or her favorite scripture passages and continue the practice, especially daily if possible, thus developing a habit of *lectio divina*. Another approach to daily *lectio* is to choose one book of the scriptures and continue reading from it consecutively.[6] Again, the point of *lectio divina* is not how much of the sacred text is covered, but that our engagement with the text leads us to insight, prayer, and communion with God.

One reminder: before beginning each *lectio*, we must place ourselves in a context of outer and inner silence. This is absolutely indispensable for the prayer.

NOTES

1. Rule of Saint Benedict, chap. 6 in *St. Benedict's Rule for Monasteries*, trans. from the Latin by Leonard J. Doyle (Collegeville: Liturgical Press, 1948) 20.

2. Gregory J. Polan, "*Lectio Divina*: Reading and Praying the Word of God," *Liturgical Ministry* 12 (Fall 2003) 201.

3. Max Picard, *The World of Silence*, pref. Gabriel Marcel, trans. Stanley Godwin (Wichita, Kansas: Eighty Day Press, 2002 [originally published in English by Regnery Gateway, 1952]) 223.

4. Polan, *Lectio Divina*, 198.

5. Polan, *Lectio Divina*, 202–06.

6. This is called *lectio continua*—a continuous reading of a sacred text.

 **CHAPTER 6**

Learning Silence from Lectio Divina

1. Creation: Arraying Silence

Lectio

> In the beginning when God created the heavens and the earth, the earth was a formless void and darkness covered the face of the deep, while a wind from God swept over the face of the waters. Then God said . . . . And on the seventh day God finished the work that he had done, and he rested on the seventh day from all the work that he had done. (Genesis 1:1–3a; 2:2)

Meditation

Formless void . . . darkness. What profound images of silence! In the beginning there was silence—the silence of void-nothingness and darkness-emptiness. In the beginning there was only God. Then God spoke. It only took the divine word piercing the void and darkness for the silence to become pregnant and give birth to the whole of creation. God's word is powerful—from nothingness the spoken divine word arrays creation in beauty and majesty. There is no longer nothingness, no longer chaos. Now there is everything.

Formless void . . . darkness. From this same nothingness come we humans. But we are different from all other creation—we are created in God's image. We, too, can create out of nothingness. We can create havoc or jealousy or disarray out of our thoughtless or hurtful words. We can create beauty or encouragement or hope out of our heart-ful words. Our words also array—they are extensions of ourselves into the universe. When our words are very good, we bring order to chaos and light to darkness. We ourselves can be God's creating and loving presence.

Formless void . . . darkness. There doesn't have to be nothingness in our lives, in our world. Uniting ourselves to the Divine Presence, through us God speaks divine words of comfort and healing, compassion and forgiveness. Our own goodness—implanted in us by the Divine One—brings order and tranquility to our own little corner of the world. The power to transform nothingness into the beauty of new creation lies within the power of our own pregnant words. All we need to do is allow God's divine word to be planted deep within us, to fill our personal formless void and darkness, to bring fullness and life.

Formless void . . . darkness. Such power we have to create, when we array ourselves with God and become a sacrament—a visible presence—of divine love. So much trust our creating God places in us: we are entrusted with creation and creating. The arraying silence out of which the beauty and goodness of creation comes draws us deeper into the mystery of our creating God, where we find all we need for life. The silence itself is even an arraying word, for it brings us to the poverty of our own being: apart from God we are nothing. With God, we have the power and responsibility to bring order out of chaos and light from darkness. We are most perfectly images of God when our words are used to array beauty and life. Through us God continues to order creation into sacred art. God works through us in our world today to continue to dispel the formless void and shatter the darkness.

Then God spoke the last arraying word: on the seventh day God rested. On that day God was silent—but now the silence is full of light and hope. Now we must be silent. We welcome God's presence, light, and hope.

Silence (within prayer or not) helps us array our lives: order our priorities, align our values, get at the heart of who we are and want to be. Arraying silence helps us keep focused on the real meaning of what we do and are about. It keeps us from scurrying off into unreal dreams, and at the same time it frees us to dream new possibilities.

- I most often speak the arraying word of divine creation when . . .

- Goodness is born when . . .

Prayer

Creating God,
you bring forth light and beauty
and life out of formless void and darkness. Help us humans—
made so wondrously in your image and likeness—
to respect all your creation,
to honor your presence in all that is,
to use our resources for your honor and glory.
May our silence ever be an audible word
proclaiming your majesty and glory.
Amen.

Contemplation

2. The Burning Bush: Naming Silence

Lectio

There the angel of the LORD appeared to him [Moses] in a flame of fire out of a bush; he looked, and the bush was blazing, yet it was not consumed. Then Moses said, "I must turn aside and look at this great sight, and see why the bush is not burned up." When the LORD saw that he had turned aside to see, God called to him out of the burning bush, "Moses, Moses!" And he said, "Here I am." Then he said, "Come no closer! Remove the sandals from your feet, for the place on which you are standing is holy ground." He said further, "I am the God of your father, the God of Abraham, the God of Isaac, and the God of Jacob." And Moses hid his face, for he was afraid to look at God . . . . But Moses said to God, "If I come to the Israelites and say to them, 'The God of your ancestors has sent me to you,' and they ask me, 'What is his name?' what shall I say to them?" God said to Moses, "I AM WHO I AM." He said further, "Thus you shall say to the Israelites, 'I AM has sent me to you.' " (Exodus 3:2–6, 13–14)

Meditation

Remove the sandals . . . holy ground. Such a little bit of leather, between the sole of Moses' feet and holy ground. Yet God commands Moses to take off his shoes—Moses stands before God bare-footed, naked. Through Moses' curiosity and response, this ancient man of God is moved from fear to the courage to ask God's name and then be sent on God's mission to free the Jews from slavery. Fear is dispelled in a face-to-face encounter with God because the Divine One *chooses us* and invites us into Divine Presence. This, even before we know God's name! God gives us everything we need to know God and hear the divine call to each of us personally to name God in our hearts and proclaim God's intimate care and presence throughout our world. We need not wait to know God before we proclaim God's presence; God comes to us and gives us the wherewithal to be a divine instrument of silence and word spoken.

God persistently seeks us, the beloved crowning word of divine creation. Just as Moses was bidden, so must we put off our shoes as we come seeking Divine Presence. Putting off our shoes is an image prompting us to clear the clutter, to become silent. We must become naked before our God—put off all that gets in the way of seeking God, of responding to God, of distracting us from God. We must remove all that keeps us from taking precious moments of silence to hear God's invitation to listen to the divine name—an act of incredible intimacy—spoken to us.

Remove the sandals . . . holy ground. In ancient times, names revealed something of who a person is or someone's mission. When God revealed the divine name I AM to Moses, God was revealing the very Godself, divinity. God chooses to make known the divine majesty to us humans—God's mere creation. But in that generous act God makes possible a sublime relationship between us creatures and our Creator. Such a small thing—to put off anything that gets in the way of such a sublime relationship.

God's revelation of the divine name (really, a revelation of the divine self) is a wholly new thing. Creatures that are distant from God are invited into Intimate Presence. All we need do is put off anything that keeps us from hearing God's voice call to us. The subsequent silence is a naming silence drawing us into knowing God more deeply than ever before. The silence carries us from fear to courage, from knowing God one way to knowing God even more in myriads of life-giving ways. We cannot carry forth God's mission if we do not know God, if we cannot name God. We cannot—because without naming God we have no relationship with God. We run the risk of the mission being other than God's mission, which is nothing less than the divine desire for our salvation—for freedom and eternal life.

- In order to encounter and name God, I must . . .

Prayer

Generous God,
you attract us to your Divine Presence in the most unexpected ways
and then each time reveal yourself anew to us.
Help us to recognize whatever it is in us or around us
which distracts us from hearing your voice.
Receive our grateful and filled hearts,
overwhelmed by your desire for intimate relationship with us.
May our silence proclaim your love for us.
Amen.

Contemplation

3. Sabbatical Year: Resting Silence

Lectio

Every seventh year you shall grant a remission of debts. . . . If there is among you anyone in need, a member of your community in any of your towns within the land that the LORD your God is giving you, do not be hard-hearted or tight-fisted toward your needy neighbor. You should rather open your hand, willingly lending enough to meet the need, whatever it may be. . . . Every firstborn male born of your herd and flock you shall consecrate to the LORD your God; you shall not do work with your firstling ox nor shear the firstling of your flock. You shall eat it, you together with your household, in the presence of the Lord your God year by year at the place that the LORD will choose. (Deuteronomy 15:1, 7–8, 19–20)

Meditation

Every seventh year . . . open your hand. . . . Only every seventh year? What a good deal. But wait: seven is a symbolic number recalling completion, fulfillment. On the seventh day of creation God rested in order to bask with pleasure at the goodness and beauty brought forth. Every seventh year (and, in a lesser way every seventh day, and in a really big way every fiftieth year) we are to be particularly conscious of our duties to others, making sure relationships are in order. Every seventh year we begin afresh and are to see others in the same way God sees us. Every seventh year (yes, even every seventh day) we are to enter into a resting silence during which we celebrate the fullness and fulfillment of all that is and all we have been given.

Observing Sabbath's resting silence is an important spiritual discipline. The rest and the time to set things and relationships right is a reminder that who we are and what we have are really not ours; everything is from God and God's graciously generous goodness. Occasionally we must welcome resting silence to remind ourselves that the world is not coming to fulfillment because of our efforts, but because God remains present in our world through us. Sabbath's rest is a way to remind ourselves of exactly how dependent we are upon God; resting silence expresses concretely and regularly our ultimate dependence on God. Resting silence is our way of saying back to God, thank you.

Only resting silence puts into perspective possessions and wealth and needs and deficiency. Without this perspective we can easily pursue what ultimately will not make us happy nor provide us with meaning. So many people spend so much time acquiring things, when we really need to spend time acquiring the resting silence which sets right our relationships. Resting silence makes sure that we don't make ourselves the center of our universe.

- I need rest when . . .

- I choose rest when . . .

- Rest is a spiritual discipline which benefits me most when . . .

Prayer
Gracious God,
you rested and took satisfaction in your creation on the seventh day.
Help us to relish rest
so that we can become even more aware of your blessings.
Help us to be mindful of others
and to reach out to those in need
with your generosity and care.
May our resting silences bring us gratefully to you.
Amen.

Contemplation

4. Samuel's Call: Listening Silence

Lectio

Now the boy Samuel was ministering to the LORD under Eli. The word of the LORD was rare in those days; visions were not widespread.

At that time Eli, whose eyesight had begun to grow dim so that he could not see, was lying down in his room; the lamp of God had not yet gone out, and Samuel was lying down in the temple of the LORD, where the ark of God was. Then the LORD called, "Samuel! Samuel!" and he said, "Here I am!" and ran to Eli, and said, "Here I am, for you called me." But he said, "I did not call; lie down again." So he went and lay down. The LORD called again, "Samuel!" Samuel got up and went to Eli and said, "Here I am, for you called me." But he said, "I did not call you, my son; lie down again." Now Samuel did not yet know the LORD, and the word of the LORD had not yet been revealed to him. The LORD called Samuel again, a third time. And he got up and went to Eli, and said, "Here I am, for you called me." Then Eli perceived that the LORD was calling the boy. Therefore Eli said to Samuel, "Go, lie down; and if he calls you, you shall say, 'Speak, LORD, for your servant is listening.'" So Samuel went and lay down in his place. (1 Samuel 3:1–10)

Meditation

The word of the Lord was rare . . . your servant is listening. In our own day it seems like the word of the Lord is likewise rare, or at least we think so because, perhaps, we don't seem to be listening or we don't perceive desired effects. Samuel teaches us to wait on the Lord's word and to persevere in listening for the divine word. Three times the Lord called to Samuel. God speaks to us, too, and speaks just as often. We can misinterpret the call of the Lord (like Samuel did at first), or we can even close our ears and not listen at all. Neither response brings us closer to the Lord.

Three times Samuel misunderstood the call because Samuel "did not yet know the LORD." Like Samuel, our own task is to try again and again to encounter the Lord so we can get to know God's presence and listen to the divine word spoken so personally to each of us. Listening silence enlarges our capacity to get to know the Lord. Personal relationship with the Divine comes from perseverance and waiting. The Lord calls, we know not when. The Lord reveals the Divine Self, we know not when. But we do know when we are able to listen: when we enter into a silence that calms our fears and perks our power to listen and discern. Developing the habit of listening for God's word is also a way of developing a habit of getting to know God's presence to us.

The word of the Lord was rare . . . your servant is listening. We hear so many words today that it is easy to be quite selective in listening. We tend to stop and listen to what pleases us, and to tune out what might challenge, bore, or demand too much of us. Perhaps it's from a perspective of self-defense that we sometimes tune out God because we know to listen and obey God is to be challenged to change, to grow, to let go of our existing desires and life patterns and place ourselves in God's hands to mold and shape as the divine will intends for us. Maybe we avoid listening silences because a listening stance may lead us where we wish not to go.

The word of the Lord was rare . . . your servant is listening. Having the posture of a servant is directly connected with improving our capacity to listen. A good servant is always ready, waiting to hear a voice calling. A good servant spends self for the good of another. Listening silence transforms us into good servants because it is practice in waiting, so that we can be more open to God's word and carry it out. It is not enough simply to *listen* to God's word; we must also act upon it. This is why God's word is so dangerous—it demands something of us. Ultimately, it demands that we hand ourselves over to God.

- I listen best when . . .

- I hear God's word best when . . .

- I am able to respond to God's word when . . .

Prayer

Holy God,
you call us to speak to us in the silent recesses of our hearts.
Help us to calm ourselves
in order to hear your word.
Help us to be true servants of your word,
leading others to know you
and the loving care of your Divine Presence.
Amen.

Contemplation

5. Elijah's Journey: Whispering Silence

Lectio

He said, "Go out and stand on the mountain before the LORD, for the LORD is about to pass by." Now there was a great wind, so strong that it was splitting mountains and breaking rocks in pieces before the LORD, but the LORD was not in the wind; and after the wind an earthquake, but the LORD was not in the earthquake; and after the earthquake a fire, but the LORD was not in the fire; and after the fire a sound of sheer silence. . . . "Then the LORD said to him. . . . " (1 Kings 19:11–15)

Meditation

Sound of sheer silence. We are used to seeking the Lord when God performs mighty deeds in great power and majesty. Elijah is standing on Mount Horeb as the word of the Lord commands him, waiting for the Lord to pass by. First three mighty nature events happen: great wind, earthquake, fire. It is not in these that Elijah finds God. Perhaps this is so because there has been so much violence in Elijah's pursuit of justice on God's behalf. God's people have strayed; they fall silent when faced with choosing Baal's prophets or Elijah. They have forsaken the covenant. Elijah has killed Baal's false prophets and now is fleeing for his own life. So much violence!

Sound of sheer silence. Not in violence or a cosmic display of might, but in the sound of sheer silence does Elijah encounter God. In sheer silence—the opposite of violence and infidelity—is the tiny whisper of God's voice assuring Elijah that God will be triumphant after all. Sometimes might distracts us from fidelity; whispering silence gently calls us faithfully to listen for God in unexpected ways. Sometimes it is only gentle, whispering silence that can salve our fears and turn us back on the journey of fidelity.

Sound of sheer silence. God does pass by in cosmic displays of might. But often it is in the gentle whisper of silence that God stays to speak a reassuring word to us, comforts us, sends us comforted and encouraged on our journey-mission. Whispering silence is really a shouted word, because whispering silence jolts us into listening for God's word. The sound of sheer silence is startling because it is the unexpected. Silence doesn't sound, except when it is God's word that breaks the silence. This whispering silence prepares us to hear God's word—which is even more startling and unexpected, because it is the sound of sheer silence.

- When seeking God, I tend to look . . .

- I most easily find God and hear the divine word addressed to me when . . .

Prayer

Gentle God,

you whisper to us in the silence of our steadfast and faithful hearts.

Help us to seek you in the sound of sheer silence.

Help us to be faithful to you,

listen to your word,

and then live as people who have embraced a covenantal relationship with you.

Amen.

Contemplation

6. Job's Righteousness: Testing Silence

Lectio

". . . But stretch out your hand now, and touch all that he has, and he will curse you to your face." The LORD said to Satan, "Very well, all that he has is in your power; only do not stretch out your hand against him!" So Satan went out from the presence of the LORD. (Job 1:11–12)

Meditation

Stretch out your hand. How miscalculating Satan is of Job's character! Job is a man of family, health, happiness, and means. He's got it all. By anyone's judgment at that time, Job was truly a man blessed by God. How miscalculating Satan is! He judges that Job is blameless and upright, altogether faithful to God, only because God has blessed him with family and possessions. Satan's taunt: take it away and see how faithful Job is. So God accepts Satan's challenge: he can take away everything, except don't lay a finger on Job.

Stretch out your hand. This, Satan does. Job loses property, family, and even his health. His friends turn against him and try to make him forsake God. In all this, nonetheless, Job is faithful: he laments his losses, but never forsakes God. Job is faithful. God, one; Satan, zero!

Stretch out your hand. Satan could take away the things of Job's life, but Satan could not take away or shake Job's fidelity. Through all of Satan's stretching out the hand of destruction and evil, God's hand of protection and goodness still enveloped Job. No matter what confronts us, we can remain faithful to God if we but keep our eyes on God because God will never forsake us, either. Things we possess are not so important as is our faithful relationship to God. In that Job was unwavering. And in the end his blessings were restored twofold.

Stretch out your hand. Whose stretched hand do we receive? All our life two hands reach out to us. God's divine hand is always there to clasp our own hand and to lead us on the path of truth and goodness. However, we are weak and fallen humans. The other hand of temptation is always stretched out to mislead us and to lead us on the path of infidelity and selfishness.

Each of us is beset by testing silence. Whose stretched hand do we receive? Testing brings us face to face with choice: fidelity to God or self-centeredness. Testing silence is the crossroad between calamity and blessing. Two hands reach out to us; we beg for the courage to grasp the hand of God, who always strengthens us to remain upright and blameless. The hand of God is steady and firm, leading us aright as we journey through testing silence. Testing silence sharpens our choices about who we want to be and how we wish to deepen our relationship with God. Testing silence beckons us to blessing or taunts us toward ruin.

- The stretched hand I reach out to grasp is . . . when . . .

- What helps me make right choices during testing silence is . . .

Prayer

Loving and kind God,
you stretch out your mighty but gentle hand
to lead us on a life-long, faithful journey of truth and goodness.
Help us to recognize all the tending care you shower upon us
to help us make good choices so we can always be upright and
      blameless before you.
Help us one day to enjoy everlasting happiness with you,
the ultimate end of our faithful journey.
Amen.

Contemplation

7. The Soul Waits: Trusting Silence

Lectio

For God alone my soul waits in silence;
> from him comes my salvation.
He alone is my rock and my salvation,
my fortress; I shall never be shaken.

How long will you assail a person,
> will you batter your victim, all of you,
> as you would a leaning wall, a tottering fence?
Their only plan is to bring down a person of prominence.
> They take pleasure in falsehood;
they bless with their mouths,
> but inwardly they curse. *Selah* [pause]

For God alone my soul waits in silence,
> for my hope is from him.
He alone is my rock and my salvation,
> my fortress; I shall not be shaken.
On God rests my deliverance and my honor;
> my mighty rock, my refuge is in God.
Trust in him at all times, O people;
> pour out your heart before him;
God is a refuge for us. *Selah*

Once God has spoken;
> twice I have heard this:
that power belongs to God,
> and steadfast love belongs to you, O Lord.
For you repay all
> according to their work. (Psalm 62:1–8, 11–12)

Meditation

My soul waits in silence. How many of us as children haven't stood in the driveway waiting for our grandparents' visit for a holiday or birthday, eagerly anticipating their hugs and kisses (and, yes, gifts)? We can fondly remember the feelings when awaiting the arrival of a good friend whom we haven't seen for a while. The heart (soul) is different during this kind of trusting waiting: we feel a buoyancy, joy, lightheartedness. Whatever of life's cares and worries may weigh us down, for those moments of immediate anticipation, cares and worries tend to lift off our shoulders and be replaced with the buoyancy of our expectation. The waiting is a trusting silence lifting us wholly out of ourselves toward the other. Even before the expected arrival, there is a communion of souls. Love binds.

My soul waits in silence. Waiting silence is always a trusting silence. When love binds, it is impossible to think that the other would not come, would be distracted by another interest. When there is serious reason for not arriving—perhaps an auto accident—there is more than the new worry about a tragedy and healing. Now there is the heartsick severance of time together, renewing friendship or relationship, strengthening bonds long since cemented. Waiting implies trust—that the other will come because of the bonds which have been established. Waiting unfolds in trusting silence. Even when there may be noise and bustle surrounding the one waiting, there is still silence—the inner unshakable love and sureness of presence.

My soul waits in silence. How much more palpable is the trusting silence when we are waiting on the Lord! The psalmist's yearning for the Lord's presence brings forth from the heart two words which aptly capture our trust in the Lord: *rock, fortress.* These are mighty images, strong images, eternal images. Rocks and fortresses are not by nature transitory, so unlike the "leaning wall" (Psalm 62:4) or "tottering fence" (Psalm 62:4) used to identify the psalmist's untrustworthy and assaulting opponents. It is so clear to whom we direct our trusting silence and eager waiting: toward the one who unfailingly will come—to God, our rock and fortress, our lover.

My soul waits in silence. The New Revised Standard Version Bible psalm translation includes an untranslatable Hebrew word, *selah* (twice in Psalm 62). Scholars differ on what this word means (it appears in other psalms, too), but many scholars presume it meant that there would be a pause for prayer inserted at these points in the psalms. It is telling in Psalm 62 that a *selah* occurs after the strophe (psalm stanza), lamenting the deplorable behavior of the enemies of the psalmist (and, therefore, of God), as well as after the stanza where the psalmist bids us to have trust in God (v. 9). It is as though the psalm is saying, first, pause (arresting silence) to consider who are victimizers and, second, pause (trusting silence) to be strengthened by God's fidelity.

My soul waits in silence. What a wonderful way to pray—just to wait on God! We build our trust in God's fidelity by this kind of joyful and sure waiting. Trusting silence strengthens our bonds of love with God (and each other) and draws us out of ourselves toward another in such a way that we burst the bounds of our own selves to become lost in another.

- When I am anticipating the visit of a loved one, I feel . . .

- When I settle myself in prayer to wait on God, I feel . . .

Prayer
Trustful God,
you patiently and faithfully await our turning toward you.
Be with us in our waiting;
assure us of your rock-like strength and fortress-like protection.
Help us to strengthen our loving bonds with you,
and thus be more ready to reach out to others with your love,
       compassion, and mercy.
Amen.

Contemplation

8. Wisdom Speaks: Discerning Silence

Lectio

> There is a rebuke that is untimely,
> and there is the person who is
>   wise enough to keep silent.
> How much better it is to rebuke
>   than to fume!
> And the one who admits his
>   fault will be kept from failure.
> Like a eunuch lusting to violate a girl
>   is the person who does right
>   under compulsion.
> Some people keep silent and are
>   thought to be wise,
>   while others are detested for
>   being talkative.
> Some people keep silent because
>   they have nothing to say,
>   while others keep silent
>   because they know when to speak.
> The wise remains silent until the
>   right moment,
>   but a boasting fool misses the
>   right moment. (Sirach 20:1–7)

Meditation

Some people keep silent because. Discerning silence helps us not only to be right, but to be right at the right moment. Discernment means prayerful choices about what to do or not to do. Discernment is different from simply a pause to think about what is being said or determining a choice. Discernment opens us to the presence of the Spirit of God, all-wise and all-knowing, who guides us in doing right at the right moment.

Some people keep silent because. This passage from the deuterocanonical book Sirach takes the perspective of one who is to rebuke another. The perspective of Sirach might be better captured for us by the familiar paraphrase "Think before you speak." All of us have had the unfortunate experience (sometimes hurtful, sometimes embarrassing, sometimes just a good laugh) of saying something we regret. Just taking a moment before we say something can often end up much more pleasant. The scripture passage then continues, essentially saying the wise person knows when and what to say and when to keep silent. The wise person practices discerning silence.

Some people keep silent because. The other side of this passage addresses the viewpoint of the person being rebuked. None of us likes to be corrected or told about something not quite right about ourselves. The bigger the flaw, the more difficult it is to face it. Our natural tendency is to get defensive and try to explain away the flaw. Discerning silence can be practiced by those on the receiving end of rebukes, as well. Discerning silence helps us hear what the other person is truly saying and judge for ourselves the truth in what's being said. Discerning silence helps us to listen to ourselves through the eyes and words of others, learn about ourselves, and prayerfully choose to change and become even better persons.

Some people keep silent because. It is not always appropriate to keep silence, and sometimes it is. Discernment helps us know when to speak and when to hold our tongue. Discerning silence is that in-between pause—making the decision to speak or not—when we decide what is the more prudent thing to do. Discerning silence opens us to another and to ourselves. Discerning silence ultimately is about healing broken relationships or strengthening solid ones. Discerning silence is really about the other.

- I most often say what I shouldn't when . . .

- I'm drawn to say what I should (even difficult things) when . . .

- I most easily practice discerning silence when . . .

Prayer

Wise and all-knowing God,
you teach us to speak rightly and to listen carefully.
Be with us in our communication with others
and help us to speak with wise minds and charitable hearts.
Help us to grow in our love for others,
for through our loving others we are loving you.
Amen.

Contemplation

9. Israel's Help: Strengthening Silence

Lectio

> Listen to me in silence, O coast lands;
>   let the peoples renew their strength;
> let them approach, then let them speak;
>   let us together draw near for
>   judgment. . . .
> . . . do not fear, for I am with you,
>   do not be afraid, for I am your God;
> I will strengthen you, I will help you,
>   I will uphold you with my
>   victorious right hand. (Isaiah 41:1, 10)

Meditation

Listen to me in silence . . . I will uphold you. How comforting are God's words through the prophet. This passage is from Isaiah; the prophet is preaching at a time when King Cyrus has overthrown Babylon and the exiled Jews are anticipating returning to their homeland. Of course, they listen to their God. The people are eager for the word that they can return. Of course they listen. Of course they take courage and strength from God. They are going home. Finally! They know this with all their heart, because God has upheld them in the past with divine strength. They *know* God's utter fidelity from repeated experience. God knows Israel's persistent infidelity from repeated experience as well.

Listen to me in silence . . . I will uphold you. The people are admonished to *listen.* They are to quiet their protests of innocence and exile and drudgery in a foreign land. They are to listen in silence, and in the silence they are challenged by the prophet: only after the silence do they dare approach God and speak. What do they speak? They speak the truth of their own infidelity to the covenant, how often they have refused God's strength and protection, how often they have relied on their own naive power rather than God's sure strength. They speak the truth, then await judgment.

Listen to me in silence . . . I will uphold you. The people are invited by God to come close and not fear. Their memory tells them that God is compassionate and merciful. Their memory reminds them that God is just. Their memory retrieves from the recesses of their sinful past the assurance that God will still love them and care for them. Israel can afford to listen to God, because there is no way to go except back home to God. With God is strength and fearlessness.

So it is with us. At times in our lives we are all exiles, we all step away from our covenantal relationship with God, weakening it until we, too, cry out and beg for God to uphold us with the divine, victorious right arm. All of us at

89

times must pause to listen to God's judgment so we can hear our exile silences as strengthening silences. Strengthening silences are those which bring us near to God, enable us to accept judgment for our weaknesses and times of failure, and open ourselves to be embraced by our loving God.

Only by opening ourselves to strengthening silence and righting our relationship with God when we stray can we also be in right relationship with each other. Strengthening silence not only brings God close to us; it also brings us closer to each other. Strengthening silence affects all our relationships, and in the end is essential if we are to be a people of covenanted community.

- Times when I have felt exiled from God are . . .

- Times when I have felt God's strength helping me are . . .

- Exile from God affects my relationship with others in that . . .

Prayer

Strong and mighty God,
you come near us with gentleness and compassion.
Help us to listen to you
and to face honestly whatever estranges us from you.
Help us to be your holy people who draw close to you
and receive strength and resolve from your goodness.
Amen.

Contemplation

10. Word Made Flesh: Glorifying Silence

Lectio

In the beginning was the Word, and the Word was with God, and the Word was God . . . And the Word became flesh and lived among us, and we have seen his glory, the glory as of a father's only son, full of grace and truth. (John 1:1, 14)

Meditation

We have seen his glory. Christians believe that from the beginning, the Word was one with the Creator. From the beginning, the Word has shared in divine glory. It was a word of God which uttered forth the world from darkness and chaos; it was the Word of God who entered into this world as a humble babe, and yet had the power and glory to dispel the darkness and chaos of sin. As in the beginning of creation there was silence because there was nothing, and then God's mighty word broke the silence to utter forth all of creation, so too at the appointed time God spoke the Word who became flesh, one like us in all things except sin.

We have seen his glory. God speaks and creation bursts forth. God speaks another Word and redemptive glory dwells among us. But even more. Saint John proclaims in the Prologue to his Gospel account that in Jesus we see the glory of God. This is mystery—that the Divine One chooses to dwell among us. An even greater mystery is that by being present to us (and within us), God's Word also raises us up to share in that same glory. We might revel in the magnificence of the color panoply of a glorious sunset, but we know that it will be short-lived; the sunset is not who we are. To revel in the glory of the Word made flesh, we also glory in our own being, for we have been touched by God's Word and re-created in a new image of God—the Word made flesh.

We have seen his glory. The glorifying silence anticipating the utterance of God's word and Word is a silence so profound and splendiferous that it transforms us, too. We ourselves share in the glory of God so much that we become refulgent with God's very glory. We encounter scintillating divine speech.

God's Word is a personal word that transforms us. A good at-hand comparison is the delighted splendor of a child's face when, for example, a parent comes home from a long trip and sweeps the child up in his or her arms. Glorifying silence is similar: it sweeps us up in the glory of God and brings us delight, wonder, awe. Glorifying silence reduces us to wide-eyed wonder at God's goodness and graciousness toward us. Glorifying silence is the resplendent fullness out of which all that is, comes. It is the fullness out of which we are re-created as God's beloved sons and daughters.

- I experience God's glory surrounding me when . . .

- I radiate that same glory when . . .

Prayer
Glorious God of the universe,
your Word was made flesh and dwelt among us,
and through that Word we share in your divine glory.
Help us always to radiate your goodness and splendor in all that we do,
no matter how seemingly small and insignificant the task.
Amen.

Contemplation

11. Jesus' Prayer: Grieving Silence
Lectio

At that time Herod the ruler heard reports about Jesus; and he said to his servants, "This is John the Baptist; he has been raised from the dead, and for this reason these powers are at work in him." For Herod had arrested John, bound him, and put him in prison on account of Herodias, his brother Philip's wife, because John had been telling him, "It is not lawful for you to have her." Though Herod wanted to put him to death, he feared the crowd, because they regarded him as a prophet. But when Herod's birthday came, the daughter of Herodias danced before the company, and she pleased Herod so much that he promised on oath to grant her whatever she might ask. Prompted by her mother, she said, "Give me the head of John the Baptist here on a platter." The king was grieved, yet out of regard for his oaths and for the guests, he commanded it to be given; he sent for and had John beheaded in the prison. The head was brought on a platter and given to the girl, who brought it to her mother. His disciples came and took the body and buried it; then they went and told Jesus.

Now when Jesus heard this, he withdrew from there in a boat to a deserted place by himself. (Matthew 14:1–13a)

Meditation

Deserted place by himself. The Gospel gives us some glimpses of the kind of relationship that existed between John the Baptist and Jesus. Even in the womb, there was leaping response by John as the two mothers, Elizabeth and Mary, met and greeted each other. John baptized Jesus. John transferred the allegiance of his own disciples to Jesus, whom he recognized as one greater than he. Related as cousins, they were also related as prophet and teacher—two inspired preachers whose lives were focused on bringing people back to covenantal fidelity with God. We don't know if there was an actual friendship between them, but this Gospel passage indicates there must have been.

After Jesus heard about John's untimely and wrongful death, he withdraws to a deserted place to be by himself. This is one of the few times in the Gospel (another clear example is over the death of Lazarus) when we experience profound grieving on the part of Jesus. Jesus' heart was so filled with love that when his own heart is pierced at John's death, the love is expressed as grieving.

Deserted place by himself. Most often at the death of a loved one, we desire to have those close to us near us. We fill the time and silences with memories—telling stories of the deceased person, attempting to keep and make fresh memories of

93

the person's life. This is how the life of another never really passes away—we are able to keep the deceased loved one fresh in our memories. We might surmise that Jesus must have shared something of his memories and feelings for John with his mother, with his disciple-friends. But then there came a time for silence. Jesus went off by himself to a deserted place to grieve.

Deserted place by himself. Grieving silence helps us release memories and make new ones. Grieving silence helps us sort through all the times with the deceased and clutch those most important memories (the ones that define a person for us) we never want to forget. Grieving silence helps us begin a process of discovering a whole new relationship we might now have with the deceased individual—one that is not a physical presence, to be sure, but nonetheless a relationship cemented by kindred spirits and common destiny.

Deserted place by himself. Grieving silence also helps us to let go of any "baggage" we still might have with the deceased person, and heal any hurts. In this healing process the self is able to cross over the gulf between now and eternity and, rather than being absent, the loved one becomes present in a new way.

The Gospel gives us no clue about what took place during Jesus' grieving over John's death. As relatives, when the families got together, Jesus and John must have spent time playing together as boys growing up. Did they get into the usual boyhood tussles? Did they play aggressively and end up with scraped knees? Was their lingering pain about not spending enough time together as adults, each instead going about his own mission? No doubt, as Jesus went off to a deserted place by himself, these and many other incidents and issues must have raced through his mind. In his own grieving silence, Jesus could come to see John in a new light and love him with a new tenderness. In the deserted place Jesus became whole again and could once again resolutely set forth on his own saving mission, knowing full well that he would suffer a similar fate as John the Baptist—a light snuffed out before its time.

- I grieve most deeply for my deceased loved ones when . . .

- I grieve for my lost memories when . . .

Prayer

God of life and goodness,
you are with us to comfort and heal us
when we grieve over the loss of our loved ones.
Help us to be healed by our good memories
and to grow in strength and resilience,
so that our grieving brings us closer to you and one another.
Amen.

Contemplation

12. Drops of Blood: Willing Silence

Lectio

He came out and went, as was his custom, to the Mount of Olives; and the disciples followed him. When he reached the place, he said to them, "Pray that you may not come into the time of trial." Then he withdrew from them about a stone's throw, knelt down, and prayed, "Father, if you are willing, remove this cup from me; yet, not my will but yours be done." Then an angel from heaven appeared to him and gave him strength. In his anguish he prayed more earnestly, and his sweat became like great drops of blood falling down on the ground. When he got up from prayer, he came to the disciples and found them sleeping because of grief, and he said to them, "Why are you sleeping? Get up and pray that you may not come into the time of trial." (Luke 22:39–46)

Meditation

Not my will but yours be done. Such a few words to pack so much result. Luke doesn't belabor the difficulty Jesus had in accepting his impending death in the same way the other synoptic evangelists do. Matthew and Mark have Jesus three times begging for the disciples' support, then begging his Father in heaven to take the cup away from him. After all, who would gleefully embrace torture and death? Jesus may be divine, but he is also very human. And like every human, he struggles in face of extreme adversity.

Not my will but yours be done. Luke uses a different image to capture Jesus' self-surrender. Here Jesus only addresses his Father once, but that is enough to convey the vivid struggle to accept or to run. For Jews, blood is the seat of life—to spill blood is to be responsible for the life of the other (this is why Jews are concerned with kosher meats). In Luke's account, Jesus is in the garden—his favorite place for prayer. Here is where the struggle plays itself out: in a familiar, prayer-worn, comfortable place. Here is where Jesus faces his crisis: whose will to follow? And then Luke shows us exactly how punishing this decision was for Jesus. He uses a loaded image—it was as though sweat in the form of drops of blood flowed down his face.

Not my will but yours be done. Sweat. We've all known at some time in our lives what it is to sweat over a decision. And, yes, maybe even we did soak our clothes a little. But in using the image of sweat in the form of drops of blood, Luke is saying something even more than simply about the challenge of conformity of wills. Luke is conveying to us that *in the very decision, Jesus' life was already ebbing away.* Just to say yes to his Father, Jesus had already handed over his life. When on the cross Jesus cries, "Father, into your hands I commend my spirit"

(Luke 23:46; the only Gospel placing these particular words on Jesus' dying lips), the "not my will but yours be done" is brought full circle and finalized. The "into your hands" of Jesus' "not my will but yours be done" is manifest on the cross where Jesus is faithful until the end. He never abandons his Father and the mission given him nor sets aside the Father's will.

Not my will but yours be done. Willing silence is that silence in which we can receive God's (or angels') ministering touch of strength. It is the blink of a pause during which we stop struggling with our fidelity in doing God's will and submit to the will of the God of justice and compassion. When we weigh our will against God's, there can be no contrary willing silence because there is no comparison between our limited knowledge and God's infinite wisdom. Of course we know God's will only seeks good for us. But nonetheless we still struggle. We know God's will and what we should do, but we still struggle.

Not my will but yours be done. Like Jesus, whenever we have important decisions to make we must go off to a familiar, comfortable, prayer-worn place that is uniquely ours. There we must pour out ourselves in prayer to God. And when we have poured out enough—when we have emptied ourselves of all our preconceived solutions or practiced self-righteousness—when we are empty, then God comes to fill. Willing silence is the blink of a pause during which we make space for God to direct our wills and guide us in good decisions for our own life.

- I struggle most with my will not squaring up with God's will when . . .

- This struggle deepens because . . .

- I can best help myself if . . .

Prayer
Shepherd God,
you guide us to do the right thing,
and in following your will we are assured of a joyful and blessed life.
Help us to seek your will,
to empty ourselves of our own wants and desires,
and to become even more enamored with your gifts of goodness to us.
Amen.

Contemplation

13. Jesus at Trial: Saving Silence

Lectio

Now the chief priests and the whole council were looking for false testimony against Jesus so that they might put him to death, but they found none, though many false witnesses came forward. At last two came forward and said, "This fellow said, 'I am able to destroy the temple of God and to build it in three days.' " The high priest stood up and said, "Have you no answer? What is it that they testify against you?" But Jesus was silent. (Matthew 26:59–63a)

Meditation

But Jesus was silent. Who of us could keep silent in face of false testimony? Who of us doesn't even attempt to defend ourselves in face of true testimony when it portrays us in a bad light? Jesus' accusers had no idea. They thought they were testifying against someone who was destroying their traditions. Or perhaps they weren't thinking at all, but were just paid to be false. Little did they know that the temple of Jesus' body would be destroyed because of their false words, but that it would also be raised up to new glory. Would that they knew.

But Jesus was silent. This doesn't seem like a very opportune moment for Jesus to keep silent. After all, his life was on the line. Only the night before, he prayed to have this cup of suffering and death pass from him. Now might be his chance.

But Jesus was silent. He was silent because truth was on his side. Once truth is spoken or acted (which he had done his entire life), there is nothing else to do except keep silent. Jesus' very silence was the loudest rebuttal he could make. Saving silence is a most brilliant repartee—who would ever keep silent in such dire circumstances? Jesus' very silence was a veritable witness to the truth of who he is, what he preached, how he lived. His very silence shouted to the mountaintops the most profound truth of who he is: the Savior.

But Jesus was silent. Saving silence does not seek to rebuke or defend, but it seeks to announce the truth of what is. *Salvation* in its Hebrew root means "wholeness" or "well-being." We are saved when we are in the kind of relationship with God which brings us to wholeness and well-being. All is well when we immerse ourselves in God's goodness and justice. All is well when we choose God above all and everyone else. Jesus had lived his clear choice through his entire life. He demonstrated his choice so clearly in the garden the night before. Now, at trial, Jesus was simply being consistent with what he had lived. Once truth is spoken, there is nothing more to say. Jesus was silent.

- I find it difficult to speak the truth when . . .

- I have been reduced to silence when . . .

- I have chosen to remain silent when . . .

- Silence has saved me in these circumstances . . .

Prayer

God of truth and salvation,
you have always spoken the truth to your beloved people:
the truth of your commandment,
the truth of your covenantal fidelity,
the truth of your compassion and mercy.
Most profoundly,
you have spoken the truth of your love
by sending your only-begotten Son to be our Savior and brother.
Help us to open ourselves
to the wholeness and goodness of our relationship with you,
and do whatever we need in order to sustain it.
Amen.

Contemplation

14. Peter's Denial: Glancing Silence

Lectio

Then they seized him and led him away, bringing him into the high priest's house. But Peter was following at a distance. When they had kindled a fire in the middle of the courtyard and sat down together, Peter sat among them. Then a servant-girl, seeing him in the firelight, stared at him and said, "This man also was with him." But he denied it, saying, "Woman, I do not know him." A little later someone else, on seeing him, said, "you also are one of them." But Peter said, "Man, I am not!" Then about an hour later still another kept insisting, "Surely this man also was with him; for he is a Galilean." But Peter said, "Man, I do not know what you are talking about!" At that moment, while he was still speaking, the cock crowed. The Lord turned and looked at Peter. Then Peter remembered the word of the Lord, how he had said to him, "Before the cock crows today, you will deny me three times." And he went out and wept bitterly. (Luke 22:54–62)

Meditation

The Lord turned and looked. According to Matthew and Mark, three times Jesus prayed in the garden to have the cup of suffering and death pass from him. Three times he asked the disciples to pray with him. Three times the disciples fell asleep. Now, three times, Peter denies Jesus. Not all the disciples are portrayed as denying Jesus—just Peter, the rock, the one on whom Jesus would build his Church. Peter does not deny knowing Jesus simply once—that alone would have been enough. No, he denies knowing Jesus three times.

In Hebrew, the root for the word *know* is the same root as for the word that means "to have sexual intercourse." Tying these two words together by root implies they belong to the same family of meanings. Both *intercourse* and *knowledge* suggest communion, union: bodily union or union of minds. When Peter denies knowing Jesus, he denies having a union of minds (and hearts and spirits) with Jesus. He really denies a relationship with Jesus. Thus, Peter's denial is more than a fearful denial of acquaintanceship; his denial is tantamount to a denial of relationship.

The Lord turned and looked. Jesus' glance at Peter must have been unique. Our tendency would be to think of this glance as a reproof (which Peter would have deserved), and we would understand perfectly well Jesus' look. On the other hand, we might consider this glace as one of tender mercy and forgiveness. With a reproof, Peter might have felt guilty; with tender mercy and forgiveness, Peter "went out and wept bitterly." A reproof is a head matter; receiving undeserved mercy and forgiveness is a heart matter, and so Peter wept. What else could he do in face of such goodness?

The Lord turned and looked. Glancing silence need not be hurtful; it can bring truth and healing and transformation. Glancing silence is the time needed to convert from head to heart. We can all take a cue from Jesus' response to Peter. Relationships are built and strengthened by positive responses. Even though another may deserve reproof, perhaps more will be gained by offering tender mercy and forgiveness instead. Peter knew he had acted malapropos; he didn't need a glance to bring him to understand that. What Peter needed was a glance that told him he could restore the relationship, that all was not lost. Perhaps it was Jesus' glancing silence at his trial that enabled Peter to respond so enthusiastically when the risen Jesus asked him, "do you love me more than these?" Peter seems hurt that Jesus should ask him three times about loving him. Had he forgotten already that three times he fell asleep in Jesus' need, and three times he denied Jesus? Had he forgotten Jesus' glancing silence?

- Another's glance has strengthened me when . . .

- I have glanced at others in these ways . . .

Prayer
Merciful and forgiving God,
your tenderness and love toward us
know no bounds,
and you desire that not one of us be lost.
Help us to see your glances, which bring us to truth,
and to respond by drawing closer to you.
Amen.

Contemplation

15. Before the Lamb: Worshipping Silence

Lectio

Then one of the elders addressed me, saying, "Who are these, robed in white, and where have they come from?" I said to him, "Sir, you are the one who knows." Then he said to me, "These are they who have come out of the great ordeal; they have washed their robes and made them white in the blood of the Lamb. . . . When the Lamb opened the seventh seal, there was silence in heaven for about half an hour. (Revelation 7:13–14; 8:1)

Meditation

Silence in heaven. This seems almost unthinkable: silence in heaven. Heaven, we think, is filled with an endless chorus of praise and thanksgiving to God for all the divine wonders and blessings bestowed upon us. Heaven is hardly a place for silence—it is a place to fill our lungs to the fullest with the breath of the Holy Spirit and sing our hearts out to our God. Is there a place for worshipping silence?

Silence in heaven. Worshipping silence is the effect of absolute absorption in the presence of the Divine. The voice can be singing, the body can be dancing, the mind can be praising, and the soul can be worshipping—and in the midst of all this non-stillness is the utter stillness of one's being completely at rest in the Lord. All activities and sounds of worship, then, are really a face of silence when the worship is directed to our communion with God.

Silence in heaven. For about a half hour there was silence in heaven, where there is no time or space. With no time, a half hour is eternity! What is the point about this half hour of silence? This is the "time" when all the heavens are in awe at the God who reveals Divine Self to both heavenly creatures and to us here on earth. Awe brings us to silence, because in the face of something beyond us, something so deep a mystery as the Divine, something so out of our experience as standing before God in worship, all we can do is stand with our mouths and eyes and ears wide open and let our very being pour out in wonderment and reverence.

Silence in heaven. Silence is the most unfathomed praise because in the no-sound there is the fullness of our whole being emptying itself out before the majesty of the Divine. In our soundless voice all is said: we acknowledge our dependence upon God, we thank God for the many blessings bestowed upon us, we cry out for mercy because of our failings, we plead for benefits for those in need. In worshipping silence the cries of our deepest longings are sounded, the sighs of our most immediate needs are sounded, the utterances of our sincerest gratitude are sounded, the songs of our highest praise are sounded, the laments of our most acute pain are sounded. In fact, there is never silence as absence; there is always the full sound of worship.

- I long for the silent sounds of worship when . . .

- Praise wells up within me when . . .

- Gratitude wells up within me when . . .

- My soul is raised to the heavens to join in the heavenly choir when . . .

Prayer

Glorious God,
you are worthy of all praise and honor, thanksgiving and reverence.
Hear our prayers of praise and thanks.
Help us elevate ourselves to be embraced by your Divine Presence,
and to know your love and protection throughout all our lives.
Amen.

Contemplation

CHAPTER 7

Sent Silence— Spent Silence

All the great experiences of life—freedom, encounter, love, death—are worked out in the silent turbulence of an impoverished spirit. A gentleness comes over [us] when . . . [we are] quietly but deeply moved by a mature encounter; [we] become[ ] suddenly humble when [we are] overtaken by love. . . . How do we explain the rise within our hearts and spirits of this wordless, empty, but deeply stirring piety? Why this withdrawal from the teeming marketplace of facile thoughts and racy interests into this recollecting poverty of a deep, chilling stillness that invades every recess of our Being?[1]

In one way or another, underlying each of the previous chapters is this funda-ment: sacred silence is in the end a self-emptying which expresses itself in love for God, self, and others. We have tried to address the questions raised by Johannes Metz in this final chapter's lead quotation. He writes of "an impoverished spirit," a spirit emptied of self so as to be filled with the Divine; a spirit emptied of all pretenses and distractions; a spirit emptied of self so that Other and other might enter in. The "chilling stillness" that invades us is the cool breeze of an evening walk with the Lord (see Genesis 3:8). In sacred silence we pass from impoverish-ment to enrichment, from sacrilege to piety, from emptiness to fullness. In sacred silence we lose everything and gain even more. Silence is our receptive vessel for God's overflowing presence.

A traditional hallmark of spirituality is that the fulfillment God brings is never simply for ourselves. God's blessings are certainly for our sake, yes, but also so that we might become icons of God's presence in our world, proclaiming divine goodness, mercy, and forgiveness. The more we are given, the more is demanded of us (see Luke 19:26a). Silence given must be silence sent. So that in the end, when we have spent silence, we simply rest in the Lord.

It is true that there is great value just for ourselves in practicing the habit of silence. Through silence we become more focused, more gentle and kind with ourselves and others, more energized to face whatever challenges life might bring us. At the same time, the practice of silence is not simply for our own good. Or, to put it another way, the good silence brings about in ourselves always demands to spill out for the good of others as well.

We turn now by way of conclusion to two final reflections on silence: sent silence and spent silence. A fruit of silence is always mission undertaken for the good of others. But in the very end, we must simply let the silence be spent, as we ourselves are spent.

Sent Silence

I am a vowed member of a Roman Catholic congregation of women religious. When I entered religious life over four decades ago, we had a rule of silence that reigned supreme. Can one imagine gathering a few dozen 18-year-old young women together under one roof and announcing to them that they would from now on keep silence? We energetic youth quickly learned how to communicate in count-less other ways: looks, gestures, body language, etc. Oh, yes, we kept the letter of the law of silence, but hardly the spirit. We looked forward to festival days when the rule was relaxed and we could enjoy our young-women chatter again.

What has fascinated me over the years is that as I've ministered during my religious life in various ways to God's people, even though by now we no longer have an explicit rule of silence in my congregation, I have come to anticipate the luxury of silence. But more: when my ministry is most demanding, I find myself needing to take even more time to be by myself in silence. Over the years I have matured enough to understand the wisdom beneath our former rule of silence. I have also learned that my early practice of silence in religious life did make a difference in me.

I have learned so well the connection between silence and ministry or mission. There are two facets to this connection: mission needs silence to be fruitful, and life-giving silence always spills over into doing good for others.

Mission needs silence. All of us fulfill many missions during life—some of them ordinary, everyday missions; some of them more extraordinary with far-reaching religious import. The term *mission* comes from the Latin verb *mittere*, which means "to send." Our lives are filled with instances of being sent. Growing up, our mother would often send us children to the grocery to buy bread or milk. We were not to tarry, especially if we had something that needed to be refrigerated. As inconsequential as this may seem, we were children sent on a mission. Parents fulfill a decades-long mission to rear their children with the values necessary for them to lead healthy, fulfilled adult lives themselves. Those of us living a faith tradition fulfill the mission of establishing God's reign of justice and truth. Some of us have had the privilege of knowing foreign missionaries—those men and women who selflessly give their lives in order to better the living conditions and strengthen the faith of those so much less fortunate than ourselves. Indeed, all of our lives are filled with mission.

Why is silence a prerequisite for mission? Without self-filling and directing silence, mission can drain us. Our being sent can quickly evolve into a job rather than a sacred ministry and trust. Being sent on a mission by its very nature means that we spend ourselves for something or someone other than ourselves. In inconsequential missions like being sent to the grocery store, the spending of ourselves is hardly radical (although the act of generosity is no less there). In more consequential missions, the spending of self is radical and draining. It is this latter kind of mission that demands silence as its prerequisite.

Silence both prepares us for mission and sustains us in our ministry. It is important to understand, then, that silence is not a once-and-for-all event. It is so closely connected to mission that silence is one of the hallmarks of caring for others. When the apostles returned to Jesus after being sent forth on mission (see, for example, Mark 6:7), Jesus invited them to "Come away to a deserted place all by yourselves and rest a while" (Mark 6:31). Resting by ourselves opens us to being filled with renewed commitment, energy, enthusiasm. It creates the space for us to rest in the Lord who sustains, nourishes, and cares for us.

Mission, however, is not only for religious apostles, for the "professional" missionaries who go to foreign lands and people to spread the Good News of God's love and compassion. At least three features of mission remind us that all of us, in little ways and bigger ways, are on mission to bring God's creation to completion.

First, mission draws us out of ourselves so we can grow beyond who we are. If silence and even our very lives is only for ourselves, then we soon become solipsistic individualists, living only for our own desires and pleasures. How quickly having more satisfies less, and we become bored with the simple delights of everyday living. By taking up our common mission to care for others—those near us such as our own family members, but also those far from us in need—we are drawn out of ourselves into a bond with all of life and humanity. Our world view and horizons are broadened by mission in such a way that ever new possibilities are presented. And it is precisely these possibilities that stretch us beyond ourselves to the discovery of ourselves in ever new ways, enabling us to reach fuller potential as gifted beings.

Second, mission connects us with others and seals our relationships with them. Human beings are not meant to live in isolation. Consider the human infant: of all the mammals, the human is the least capable at birth of sustaining its own life and takes the longest to become independent. We lament the breakdown of families and neighborhoods in our society because instinctively we know that the best in ourselves develops as we are in relation to others. Mission fosters community and is deepened by the life silence offers. In contrast, isolation grows out of non-relationship and empty silences.

A third feature of mission is that we continue God's creative act and share in the blessings and joy of all that is good. God did not create a world that was polished, finished, fixed. God's creative desire is to break open a never-ending process of growth and life. When we take up a mission to relate to others, we are contributing to bringing to fulfillment what God had begun at the very beginning of time. As creatures made in the Creator's image, mission is one way we express in the here and now how like God we truly are. As creation itself happened out of the silence of void and darkness, so does our mission to better our world happen out of silence—but now a silence filled with Divine Presence that fills us and sends us forth.

Silence spills over. We often read in newspapers or hear media commentaries on the self-centeredness of our society. Yet people are capable of heroic generosity and self-giving. I prefer being an optimist: there are far more generous people around us than selfish people. Those who so generously respond to the needs of others do so out of a well of silence. Further, the most profound sacred silence—the kind of silence which mediates Divine Presence—cannot be contained. It wells up within us and thrusts us outward toward others, affording us an opportunity to share our spirituality—our very life—with others.

The spilling over of sacred silence has its dangers. When we speak the truth of Divine Presence, others may mock us, scorn us, banish us. We risk becoming as unpopular as the prophet Jeremiah. We may, with Jeremiah, be tempted to say, "I will not mention him [God], or speak any more in his name," but then, also like Jeremiah, "within me there is something like a burning fire shut up in my bones; I am weary with holding it in, and I cannot" (Jeremiah 20:9). It seems like the genuine habit of sacred silence leaves us in a real bind. On the one hand, it makes such demands on us that we grow weary of being sent on mission to further God's reign. On the other hand, if we want to quit our mission, the silence wells up within us so that we seem ready to burst. The silence itself seems to supply us with the strength to carry forward God's will and take up once again our participation in the divine mission to bring all humanity and creation back in relationship with God.

In all the great religious traditions, God has called prophets and seers, disciples and missionaries to spread the truth of divine blessings. Encounters with the Divine One and growing awareness of divine goodness are not to be clutched to oneself, but beg to be shared. In this way God's ways become known within us and our silences; as well, they are made available through us to all the world. Silence can be kept and savored only for a time. Then we must break our silence and speak, so that through our utterances others might come to the kind of silence that brings them into God's presence. To receive God into us means we have an accompanying responsibility to share God beyond us, among those we meet in our families, work places, times of leisure. We are all called to be both disciples and missionaries of the God in whom we believe and are drawn to adore.

Silence's proclivity to send us forth does not mean we must become door-thumping proselytizers. We do not have to *speak* about silence in order for its value and the depth of the Divine within us to be conveyed to others. It does mean that the habit of silence becomes so much a part of our everyday living that others can benefit from the peace and calm, the centeredness and aliveness which emanate from us. And perhaps this is our most challenging mission: simply to be ourselves.

When we develop the habit of silence, something happens to us. We naturally become more attentive to others, we pick up on needs quicker, we are aware of our surroundings and what may be out of kilter much more keenly. This is, remember, because silence empties us of our own inordinate self-concern and focuses us outside of ourselves. This out-reach, this outward focus, is sent silence, is silence's mission.

In our missionary activity, we must have the eagerness of Isaiah ("Here am I; send me!" [Isiah 6:8b]) and the reluctance of Jeremiah ("Ah, Lord GOD! Truly I do not know how to speak, for I am only a boy" [Jeremiah 1:6]). Eagerness enables us to take risks and go where we would not choose, and be with those whose company we would tend not seek; reluctance give us pause, so that we are always aware that it is the Lord's work which we do.

Sent silence is not a burden if our mission truly derives from the grace of silence itself. Mission must always be our choice, and we must own the mission—its values, demands, message, impact, fruits—if we are to remain faithful to it. If mission becomes a burden, then we must retreat to silence to hear once again who we are and are called to be. We must wait on the Lord. We are sent on mission not by our voice, but by the divine voice. That divine voice is the guarantee, if we surrender to the silence and the self-emptying demands of the mission, that all will be well. God will reign and there will be everlasting joy and peace.

Reader Response Interlude

- The missions I undertake daily are . . .

- The call to mission that is serving others compels me to . . .

- My silence spills out to mission when . . .

- When ministering to others, I need silence when . . .

Spent Silence

As we ponder all the goodness that comes from the habit of silence, it is a wonder that all of us don't take ourselves off to a cloister. The value of silence would seem to entice us to be in silence all the time. Our lives, however, are not spent mostly in silence. Silence is the lavish gift of our Creator to those of us who choose to emulate divine rest. Even with the Creator, however, there was a rhythm of creating and rest. So it is with our own lives. There is a rhythm of necessary human activity and evitable rest. There is a rhythm of silence and mission.

Deep silence is always pregnant—it always gives birth to greater life. The silence reminds us that more is possible, that we are never finished, that there is always someone new to meet, something else to accomplish, another good to do. Silence is never static. It is ever dynamic, rolling over us like a great thunderstorm demanding that we pay attention and get on with more of life. At some point the silence always strains to burst outside of itself. This is spent silence: the point during silence when we've had enough, when we become restless to move on, to take up our mission, to reach out to others with the very goodness that has been given each of us.

Spent silence reminds us that we are co-creators, ever on a mission to make this world better for ourselves and others. Spent silence reminds us of the right relationship we must have with all of nature and with all others. Spent silence does not let us always be still. Spent silence is the brink of new possibilities, new discoveries, new relationship, new life. Spent silence reminds us of who we are: the crowning beings of creation, made in the Divine Creator's image, forever called to grow into the mystery of who we are.

Spent silence brings us to the brink of who we can yet become. Spent silence assures us that creation is not finished, nor is our relationship with God and others exhausted. There is ever more. Spent silence thrusts us from the cocoon of silence because the work of silence is finished and now we must burst forth. With spent silence we are brought to a new point in life, a new relationship with the sacred and ourselves, a new energy to be spent for the sake of others. Spent silence urges us to get on with life.

Reader Response Interlude

- The rhythm of silence in my own life unfolds best when . . .

- My sense of full silence bursting to be spent happens when . . .

- Spent silences energizes me to . . .

Why Sent Silence Is Spent Silence

Fruitful mission both derives from silence and returns to silence. When derived from silence, it is spent silence—it is the work which follows a silence so pregnant with energy and being that it cannot be contained. When the silence is fullest, it requires release. That release is spent silence, is mission—deeds undertaken for the good of others. But mission and ministry and work, in turn, become their own drain. And so we return to silence, to be filled once again, to refocus on who we are and what we are about. But mostly we return to silence as a necessary part of mission to ensure that the mission is not ours, but is God's work being incarnated in us.

In these seven chapters we have shared many words during our lengthy journey together into a reflection and prayer about silence as living and praying a sacred art. Together during these pages we have undertaken our own mission—to delve into the meaning and value of earthy and sacred silence. We have had opportunities—during the Reader Response Interludes and during the 15 examples of *lectio divina*—to practice silence and prayer. And now, the words must stop. Now, it is time once again to be silent.

NOTES

1. Johannes Baptist Metz, *Poverty of Spirit*, trans. John Drury (Paramus, New Jersey and New York: Newman Press, 1968) 49–50.

About the Author

Joyce Ann Zimmerman, CPPS, PHD, STD, is the director of the Institute for Liturgical Ministry in Dayton, Ohio; the founding editor (1992) and columnist for *Liturgical Ministry*; adjunct professor of liturgy at the Athenaeum of Ohio; a liturgical consultant; frequent speaker and facilitator of workshops on liturgy, spirituality, and other related topics; and an award-winning author of numerous books and articles on liturgy and spirituality. She is the recipient of the Notre Dame Center for Liturgy's 2008 Michael Mathis Award.

NOTES

NOTES